"*Jesus's Final Week* is a clear and concise study of the passion week of the Savior of the world. It is excellently written and will serve well the seasoned scholar or layperson who wants to examine the week leading up to and including the crucifixion and resurrection of Jesus Christ. I personally will take advantage of this fine work."

—**Daniel Akin**, president, Southeastern
Baptist Theological Seminary

"As a seminary student, Dr. Bill Cook was one of my favorite professors. In *Jesus's Final Week* you'll understand why. Cook writes with the accuracy of an accomplished New Testament scholar, the clarity of a gifted teacher, and the pastoral application of a seasoned minister. Reading this book will not only afford you a better understanding of Christ's final days, it will deepen your devotion to our Savior."

—**Jason Allen**, president, Midwestern
Baptist Theological Seminary

"No portion of God's Word is more fascinating than those chapters relating the final days detailing the redeeming death and resurrection of Jesus. For two millennia Christians have meditated on these painful yet glorious close-ups of the Savior. I know of no one better suited to lead twenty-first century Christians to examine the central drama of history than Dr. William F. Cook III. As a New Testament scholar, pastor, and devout man of prayer, he presents to the church a volume well-suited both for study and devotion. Ponder, then worship!"

—**Ted J. Cabal**, professor of philosophy of religion,
Southwestern Baptist Theological Seminary

"Too often, we have read about the final week of Jesus so many times that we almost skim it now. The events of that week, though, are so history-changing that we must meditate on them more. This book will help you do that. Dr. Cook carefully walks through that week, writing with the mind of a scholar and the heart of a pastor. You will learn more about the events themselves, consider practical implications and applications of the stories, and come out of each chapter singing the 'hymn of response' Dr. Cook includes. This study is worth leading your entire congregation to do."

—**Chuck Lawless**, vice president for spiritual formation and ministry centers and Richard & Gina Headrick Chair of World Missions, Southeastern Baptist Theological Seminary

"I have had the privilege to know Dr. Bill Cook for many years now in two different contexts. First, he was my faithful pastor for six years. Second, he was my esteemed colleague at The Southern Baptist Theological Seminary for fifteen years. From my unique vantage point, I can say without hesitation that Dr. Cook has the mind of a scholar and the heart of a pastor. Both of those qualities come into full view in *Jesus's Final Week*. The reality is that it would be impossible to faithfully preach the four Gospels without being well versed in Jesus's final days and the events leading up to his death, resurrection, post-resurrection appearances, and ascension. With that said, this new work has instantly become my 'go to' source for those final days leading to Jesus's ascension. As I read, my mind and heart were renewed and enthralled with the love and glory of Jesus and his all-sufficient and perfect work of redemption for all who believe."

—**Brian Payne**, pastor, Lakeview Baptist Church, Auburn, AL

"The most important event in all of history is the arrival of Jesus on this earth. And the most important week in his life is certainly his last. Bill Cook provides a simple, faithful, thorough, and meditative summary of Jesus's final week. Follow this expert guide as he leads you through the events that guide us toward salvation."

—**Patrick Schreiner**, associate professor of New Testament and biblical theology, Midwestern Baptist Theological Seminary

JESUS'S
FINAL
WEEK

JESUS'S FINAL WEEK

From
TRIUMPHAL ENTRY
to **EMPTY TOMB**

WILLIAM F. COOK III

ACADEMIC
NASHVILLE, TENNESSEE

ISBN: 978-1-0877-3755-3

Dewey Decimal Classification: 232.96
Subject Heading: JESUS CHRIST—PASSION / JESUS
CHRIST—ENTRY INTO JERUSALEM / JESUS CHRIST—
BETRAYAL AND ARREST

Printed in the United States of America
1 2 3 4 5 6 7 8 9 10 BTH 27 26 25 24 23 22

For my grandchildren:
Will, Riley, Emery, Hadley, Ainsley, Lila, and Isabel.
Thank you for the joy and happiness you bring into Papa's life!
May you love and serve Jesus, our Risen Savior,
all the days of your lives.
Love, Papa

CONTENTS

Acknowledgments   xi

Introduction   xiii

1. The Triumphal Entry   1
   Palm Sunday: April 2, AD 30

2. The Cursing of the Fig Tree and Clearing of the Temple   15
   Monday: April 3, AD 30

3. Temple Controversies and Teaching   27
   Tuesday: April 4, AD 30

4. The Betrayal of Jesus Christ   53
   "Silent" Wednesday: April 5, AD 30

5. The Last Supper   59
   Maundy Thursday: April 6, AD 30

6. The Garden of Gethsemane   81
   Thursday Night–Early Hours of Friday Morning:
   April 6–7, AD 30

7. The Jewish Trial: Guilty of Blasphemy   93
   Early Hours of Friday: April 7, AD 30

8. The Roman Trial: Guilty of Treason   109
   Friday: April 7, AD 30

9. The Crucifixion and Death of Jesus Christ   119
   Good Friday: April 7, AD 30

10. The Resurrection of Jesus Christ   143
    Sunday, April 9, AD 30

Group Study Guide   163
Name and Subject Index   182
Scripture Index   186

ACKNOWLEDGMENTS

I would like to acknowledge several people as I complete this work. After more than thirty-eight years my wife, Jaylynn, remains the love of my life. Except for the gift of salvation, she is the greatest gift the Lord has ever given me. Thank you, sweetheart, for your love and devotion to me, our family, and especially our Savior.

I am indebted to my doctoral student and Garrett Fellow, Graham Faulkner, for his research assistance. My church member and friend, Walker Downs, was a significant help by reading the manuscript and making so many helpful suggestions as well as writing the study guide.

I want to express my gratitude to Dr. R. Albert Mohler for the privilege of serving at The Southern Baptist Theological Seminary for the past twenty-one years.

Finally, I would be remiss not to express my gratitude for the kind folks at B&H. Madison Trammel, Audrey Greeson, and the editorial team have been kind and patient throughout the entire process.

INTRODUCTION

The climax of Jesus's messianic ministry began as he entered Jerusalem on Palm Sunday. He rode into the city on the back of a donkey as Israel's Messiah-King. The week when these events occurred has been called "Holy Week" throughout much of church history. Some traditions refer to this week as "Passion Week." The word "passion" comes from the Latin *passio*, meaning "suffering." I will use the terms Holy Week and Passion Week interchangeably throughout this work. Holy Week is the most important week in human history!

The four Gospels recount the events leading up to Jesus's horrific death by crucifixion and culminate with his bodily resurrection, post-resurrection appearances, and ascension. The importance of these events can be seen in the amount of space the Gospels devote to them. For example, approximately 40 percent of Mark's Gospel is dedicated to Jesus's final days (chs. 11–16); about 30 percent of Matthew (chs. 21–28); approximately 24 percent of Luke (19:28–24:53); and more than 40 percent of John (12:12–21:25). From this cursory glance, the Evangelists obviously considered the final events of Jesus's life to be of paramount importance. These events were at the center of the preaching of the early church as well (Acts 2:23–36; 3:13–26; 1 Cor 15:1–7).

One might wonder if another book on Passion Week is necessary. The publication of Eckhard J. Schnabel's *Jesus in Jerusalem: The Last Days* (Grand Rapids, MI: Eerdmans, 2018) is a monumental enterprise that in more than 600 pages addresses every important person, place, and event in Passion Week (truly an encyclopedic and magisterial work). Anyone doing extensive research on Jesus's final week will benefit greatly from its scholarly presentation. The length of the work, however, is somewhat daunting for students of the Gospels who want more of an overview of those events. An older work of even greater detail than Schnabel's is the massive two-volume tome by Raymond E. Brown, *The Death of the Messiah: From Gethsemane to the Grave* (New York: Doubleday, 1994). Brown's two volumes combined contain more than 1,600 pages without touching on the resurrection narratives! No scholar working on the Passion narratives can ignore either of these two volumes. Yet the sheer size of these works is overwhelming for many people.

A work more akin to mine is the excellent volume written by Andreas J. Köstenberger and Justin Taylor, *The Final Days of Jesus: The Most Important Week of the Most Important Person Who Ever Lived* (Wheaton, IL: Crossway, 2014). A couple of differences exist between my work and Köstenberger and Taylor's in that I do not include the full biblical text within the volume, which allows more space to discuss the events themselves. In addition, I conclude each chapter with reflections for personal application based on the day's events as well as a hymn or worship song to help you conclude your reading with worship of the Lord.

I obviously have not written this volume for the same audience as Schnabel or Brown. I have sought to write with enough detail to help you better understand what transpired throughout the week. While matters of scholarly disagreement are important to discuss, these discussions would necessarily encumber the flow of this book. For this same reason, I have not used extensive footnotes but rather have attempted a straightforward explanation of the week's events. When necessary, I use footnotes to point the interested reader to more significant discussions. There are many wonderful commentaries available on each of the four Gospels that focus great attention to details on the meaning of the biblical text. While I have consulted commentaries, and make references to them in the notes, I have sought to avoid simply writing a traditional commentary.

There are two ways to read the Gospels. The most common method is to read "vertically" through a Gospel. This approach involves reading straight through, passage by passage. A second approach is to read the Gospels "horizontally," comparing one Gospel's account with another. I am attempting to examine Jesus's final days by exploring them through a horizontal reading of the texts, based upon A. T. Robertson's *A Harmony of the Gospels*,[1] though I do diverge from his arrangement occasionally.

Jesus's Final Week can be used in several different ways. First, an individual can use this book to prepare for Holy Week. By reading the biblical texts noted in each section, and then reading through the chapter, a person can get a sense of how the week progressed for Jesus, culminating in his death and resurrection. This volume could also be useful for small groups in preparation for a church's Easter celebration. We live in a day where congregational continuity is at an all-time low. For many churches, their members see each other only once a week. Sundays are more like

---

[1] A. T. Robertson, *A Harmony of the Gospels for Students of the Life of Christ: Based on the Broadus Harmony in the Revised Version* (New York: Harper & Brothers, 1922).

believers attending a Bible conference with wonderful worship and excellent preaching and then coming back the next week and doing it again. Church leaders must be intentional if they want to bind a congregation together as a church family. At the end of the book, I have included a study guide for small groups with discussion prompts, which allows a group to study Jesus's final week together. Additionally, the hymns at the end of each chapter focus on the death of Christ. The final chapter concludes with a resurrection hymn for Resurrection Sunday. The purpose of the hymns is to allow individuals or small groups to complete the time of reading and study with worship to the Lord. The purpose of all study of Jesus's life is to love him more passionately and to serve him more faithfully.

My prayer for you is that you will fall more in love with Jesus Christ because of his substitutionary death and glorious resurrection.

CHAPTER 1

THE TRIUMPHAL ENTRY

PALM SUNDAY: APRIL 2, AD 30

Passion Week could not have begun on a bigger note! On Sunday morning Jesus and his disciples left Bethany and headed to Jerusalem.[1] This event is significant in that it is the first episode recorded by all four Gospels since the feeding of the five thousand. Up to that point in Jesus's ministry, he had sought to keep his messianic identity quiet. He would soon announce to those with eyes to see that he was Israel's long-awaited Messiah. Christians commemorate Jesus's triumphal entry into Jerusalem as Palm Sunday, which took place one week before the resurrection. The triumphal entry is the first of three prophetic acts Jesus performed at the beginning of Passion Week.

Population estimates of Jerusalem in Jesus's day vary widely. The city proper may have had between twenty-five thousand to fifty thousand inhabitants, with the larger number likely including nearby villages. During major feasts, the number would likely

---

[1] Matt 21:1–9; Mark 11:1–10; Luke 19:28–40; John 12:12–19.

swell to as many as two hundred thousand.[2] This would be especially true during Passover. One can imagine how the crowded streets made it difficult to maneuver through the city. Passover pilgrims often arrived in Jerusalem up to a week beforehand to make the necessary preparations for the feast—buy the necessary supplies and perform any required purification rituals—and to secure a location within the boundaries of Jerusalem to eat the Passover meal. While pilgrims did not normally ride into Jerusalem, Jesus was no ordinary pilgrim, and this was no ordinary entry. Before we examine Jesus's triumphal entry, it is appropriate to look back at the previous day, when Mary of Bethany anointed him. Little did those gathered that evening realize the most important week in human history was about to begin.

Mary Anoints Jesus in Bethany[3]

This event took place on Saturday evening, April 1. Jesus arrived in the village shortly before the beginning of the Sabbath on Friday, March 31.[4] At Bethany, Jesus surely was greeted by

---

[2] For a book-length treatment of Jerusalem in Jesus's day, see Joachim Jeremias, *Jerusalem in the Time of Jesus: An Investigation into Economic and Social Conditions during the New Testament Period*, trans. F. H. Cave and C. H. Cave (Philadelphia: Fortress, 1969). Although somewhat dated, it remains a helpful resource. For a recent discussion see Steve Walton, "Jerusalem," in *Dictionary of Jesus and the Gospels*, 2nd ed., ed. Joel B. Green (Downers Grove, IL: IVP Academic, 2013), 408–14.

[3] Matt 26:6–13; Mark 14:3–9; John 12:1–8.

[4] The dating of Holy Week is disputed. The two most likely years are AD 30 or 33. I believe it is slightly more probable these events took place in AD 30. If this is the case, then Jesus's triumphal entry happened on Sunday, April 2, with his crucifixion on Friday, April 7, and his resurrection on Sunday, April 9. For a discussion on the dating of the major events

friendly faces. On Saturday evening, the day before his entry into Jerusalem, a dinner was held in his honor. He had not been in Bethany since he raised Lazarus from the dead. He returned, knowing the religious leaders wanted to kill him.

Bethany was located about two miles southeast of Jerusalem. A person could walk from the village to Jerusalem in a little less than an hour. Bethany would be Jesus's home base during the week (Mark 11:1, 11, 12). Each evening he and his disciples would leave the city and return there.

The meal in Jesus's honor took place at the home of Simon the leper.[5] We do not know anything more about Simon, but we can easily see he was one of those pitiful people stricken by leprosy that Jesus healed. Only John gives the time reference, "six days before the Passover." The meal was a special banquet, considering the guests are described as reclining. Jewish people typically sat at meals and reclined on couches for special occasions. John alone includes the presence of Mary, Martha, and Lazarus.

Surprisingly, Luke is the only evangelist who does not record this anointing, although he describes a similar event, but a different anointing, earlier in his Gospel (Luke 7:36–50). Mark's placement of this event is not intended to be chronological. He places it between the plotting of the religious leaders (Mark 14:1–2) and the betrayal by Judas (vv. 10–11). Thus, the

---

in Jesus's life, see Craig L. Blomberg, *Jesus and the Gospels: An Introduction and Survey*, 2nd ed. (Nashville: B&H Academic, 2009), 225–29. For a more complete discussion of the dating of the major events in Jesus's life, see Harold W. Hoehner and Jeannine K. Brown, "Chronology," in Green, *Dictionary of Jesus and the Gospels*, 2nd ed., 134–38. Another chronological issue is to remember that for Jewish people the day began at 6 p.m. and lasted until the following evening at 6 p.m.

[5] Matt 26:6; Mark 14:3.

anointing is bracketed on each side by acts of treachery. Mark's reference "two days before the Passover" (v. 1) refers specifically to the meeting of the Jewish leadership.

The anointing was a monumental moment as evidenced by Jesus's comment, "Wherever the gospel is proclaimed in the whole world, what she has done will also be told in memory of her" (v. 9). Mary's action is one of the most moving expressions of devotion in the Bible. The description of the perfume as "very expensive" (v. 3) is an understatement. Judas estimated the value at three hundred denarii (John 12:4–5). A common laborer's daily wage was one denarius, making its value equal to about one year's salary. The perfume was imported from northern India, which contributed to its worth. "Nard" was the name of both a plant and the fragrant oil it yielded.[6] The costliness of the perfume suggests it may have been a family heirloom. The valuable perfume certainly would have been helpful to the family if they fell on hard times.

Mark indicates that Mary poured the perfume over Jesus's head, while John states she anointed his feet. The bottle contained enough for her to anoint both his head and feet. Anointing the head of a distinguished guest at a banquet was common. The anointing of the feet was quite unusual; typically, the host would provide water to wash guests' feet. In the next chapter John describes Jesus washing his disciples' feet. Mary's anointing of Jesus's feet and wiping them with her hair demonstrates her humility. Jewish women normally did not take down their hair in public, so this act adds to the shocking nature of the event. The comment about the fragrance of the aroma filling the room is an eyewitness memory (John 12:3).

---

[6] John J. Rousseau and Rami Arav, *Jesus and His World: An Archaeological and Cultural Dictionary* (Minneapolis: Fortress, 1995), 216–20.

While Judas led the way in criticizing Mary, the other disciples followed his lead quickly. The contrast between Mary and Judas is also striking. Their thoughts were completely different on this occasion. On the one hand, Mary demonstrated that no expense was too great to express her love for Jesus. Judas, on the other hand, was concerned with the financial loss. While Mary worshipped, Judas scorned and seethed over the loss of potential income into the coffer (v. 5).

John indicates that Judas was not concerned about the poor, but that he was a thief (v. 6). This comment is the first clear hint in the Gospels that Judas had a serious character flaw. Scholars debate why Judas betrayed Jesus and how it was that Satan was able to enter him (13:27). At least part of the answer is his covetousness. After Jesus's stinging rebuke, Judas approached the religious leaders asking what they would give him in exchange for Jesus (Matt 26:14–15). The fact that Judas served as the treasurer for the group suggests he was a person of some ability. Everyone must have felt he was trustworthy. Judas's fate is a striking reminder of the danger of greed and how easily it can capture a person's soul.

Jesus defended Mary against Judas's attack. The language of John 12:7 is somewhat difficult and open to various interpretations: "Leave her alone; she has kept it for the day of my burial." The most likely explanation is that Jesus implied that Mary's action was more important than even she understood. Her act of humble devotion is symbolic of his coming burial, which was something she did not comprehend. The perfume had providentially been saved for this purpose. Often, an anointing was associated with festivity; however, here, Jesus's thoughts were clearly on the cross. Thus, to those who heard his comment his words must have seemed out of place. Jesus's statement about the poor,

"For you always have the poor with you, but you do not always have me" (v. 8), certainly does not mean that he was discouraging his followers from helping the poor.[7] Rather, Jesus was saying that the events of those days were particularly significant; and, considering them, this anointing was entirely appropriate.

Judas's betrayal, which was motivated in part by greed, explains Jesus's warning, "Watch out and be on guard against all greed, because one's life is not in the abundance of his possessions" (Luke 12:15); and Paul's statement, "The love of money is a root of all kinds of evil" (1 Tim 6:10). Mary's act of extravagant devotion teaches us that sometimes extravagance for kingdom causes is the most appropriate use of our resources. Christ's church needs more people like Mary of Bethany.

We now turn our attention to the beginning of Passion Week.

Preparations for Entry[8]

Jesus and his followers left Bethany early Sunday morning to make the short journey to the city.[9] As they made their way toward Jerusalem, they approached the small village of Bethphage. Jesus sent two of his disciples to retrieve a colt for him. He gave them meticulous instructions for finding the colt and what to say if they were questioned about taking it. Their response was to be

---

[7] The Bible is filled with statements encouraging helping the poor. For example, see Prov 14:31; 19:17; 22:9.

[8] Matt 21:1–7; Mark 11:1–7; Luke 19:29–35; John 12:12–19.

[9] For a more academic discussion on the entry, see Rikki E. Watts, "Triumphal Entry," in Green, *Dictionary of Jesus and the Gospels*, 2nd ed., 980–85.

"The Lord needs it." The fact that the colt had never been used for a secular purpose made it appropriate for religious use.[10]

Scholars debate whether this event is an example of Jesus's supernatural foreknowledge or careful planning. Either is possible. On the one hand, the Gospel writers clearly describe Jesus as knowing things about people and future events that no ordinary person could possibly know. On the other hand, prearranging this event with the owner of the colt would explain his detailed instructions to his disciples and what to say if questioned. In addition, Jesus's planning also would heighten the fact that he had been preparing for this moment for some time, thereby emphasizing its symbolic significance. Either way, this event demonstrates Jesus's control of the situation. Matthew records that the disciples brought two animals to Jesus, reasoning that one of the animals was the colt Jesus rode and the other the colt's mother. The mother's presence would have provided a calming effect for an animal that had never been ridden and was suddenly surrounded by a raucous crowd.

The Fulfillment of Scripture[11]

Matthew and John indicate that Jesus's entry into Jerusalem fulfilled Zech 9:9:

> Rejoice greatly, Daughter Zion!
> Shout in triumph, Daughter Jerusalem!
> Look, your King is coming to you;

---

[10] Eckhard J. Schnabel, *Jesus in Jerusalem: The Last Days* (Grand Rapids, MI: Eerdmans, 2018), 156–57. See Num 19:2; Deut 21:3; and 1 Sam 6:7.

[11] Matt 21:4–7; John 12:14–15. See also Isa 62:11.

he is righteous and victorious,
humble and riding on a donkey,
on a colt, the foal of a donkey.

Zechariah 9:9 falls within a larger passage that describes the return of Israel's King to a restored Judah. The verse depicts the King's entry into Jerusalem. Ancient kings typically rode into cities on a warhorse. Zechariah's prophecy reveals unexpected qualities about Israel's Messiah-King. He came not to conquer by force but to offer people peace with God. Israel longed for a great militaristic messiah to rescue them from Roman domination. Even with this prophecy from Zechariah, the people failed to recognize their Messiah-King.

Another likely Old Testament connection is found in Gen 49:10–11:

The scepter will not depart from Judah
or the staff from between his feet
until he whose right it is comes
and the obedience of the peoples belongs to him.
He ties his donkey to a vine,
and the colt of his donkey to the choice vine.
He washes his clothes in wine
and his robes in the blood of grapes.

The Genesis passage is situated within a larger section where Jacob pronounced a blessing on his sons and predicted their future. One wonders why Judah was so greatly blessed; his transgressions were significant. For example, he sold Joseph into slavery and lied to defraud his daughter-in-law. We must not forget Judah's dramatic change of character when he begged Joseph to allow him to take the place of their younger brother Benjamin

(Gen 44:18–34). God chose Judah to be the ancestor of Israel's line of kings (49:10).

The Mount of Olives sits east of the Temple Mount and overlooks it, providing a beautiful panoramic view of the city. The Messiah would manifest himself to Israel there. Zechariah 14:4 reads, "On that day his feet will stand on the Mount of Olives, which faces Jerusalem on the east. The Mount of Olives will be split in half from east to west, forming a huge valley, so that half the mountain will move to the north and half to the south."

As mentioned earlier, up to this point in his ministry Jesus had sought to keep his messiahship quiet; now he openly declared himself to be the Messiah who fulfills the ancient prophecies. In similar fashion, centuries earlier, Solomon rode into Jerusalem on David's donkey to claim his throne (1 Kgs 1:32–48).

The Jubilation of the Crowd[12]

At that point the crowd began to spread garments and palm branches on the road like a red carpet. Some cried out, **"'Hosanna!' / Blessed is he who comes / in the name of the Lord"** (Mark 11:9). Mark references verses 25–26 of Psalm 118, which is part of the *Hallel* psalms.[13] These psalms were sung by pilgrims as they entered Jerusalem at festivals, such as Passover. The cry "Hosanna" may be a prayer asking God to establish his kingdom; or, by the first century, it might have been just an exclamation of joy similar to "Praise the Lord!" Others in the

---

[12] Matt 21:8–9; Mark 11:8–10; Luke 19:36–38; John 12:12–13.

[13] Pss 113–18.

crowd referred to Jesus as a prophet, some as the son of David, and still others as king.

Jesus Weeps over Jerusalem[14]

As Jesus sat on his donkey overlooking the city, he wept as he predicted its coming destruction and desolation. Sadly, and tragically, Jerusalem's rejection of Jesus would cost them dearly. Jesus explained the nature of his anguish as he described the destruction of Jerusalem that would take place in AD 70. His comment that the true meaning of these events was "hidden from [their] eyes" (Luke 19:42) indicates that their opportunity to recognize his identity had passed. Jesus used Old Testament language to describe the destruction of the city.[15] He did not merely shed a few tears over the city; he mourned deeply over its destiny. Later, he would express how often he wanted to gather the people of Jerusalem under his arms as a hen gathers her chicks for protection, but they were not willing (Matt 23:37).[16]

Jesus Enters the City to Protests and Praise[17]

Confrontation arose after Jesus entered the city. The children present in the temple precinct joined in with the crowd that

---

[14] Luke 19:41–44.

[15] See Isa 29:3; Jer 6:6–21; 52:4–5; Ezek 4:1–3.

[16] On the destruction of Jerusalem, see R. A. Guelich, "Destruction of Jerusalem," in *Dictionary of Jesus and the Gospels*, ed. Joel B. Green, Scot McKnight, and I. Howard Marshall (Downers Grove, IL: InterVarsity, 1992), 172–76.

[17] Matt 21:10–11, 14–17; Luke 19:39–40.

accompanied Jesus into the city shouting, "'Hosanna' to the Son of David" (Matt 21:15). The chief priests, scribes, and Pharisees grew irate at the adoration of the crowd. They demanded that Jesus silence them. Jesus replied, "I tell you, if they were to keep silent, the stones would cry out" (Luke 19:40). The phrase "the stones would cry out" (see Hab 2:11) is hyperbolic, suggesting that even inanimate objects understood the significance of this moment. Jesus responded to the criticism of the religious leaders by quoting from Psalm 8:2, "Yes, have you never read: **You have prepared praise from the mouths of infants and nursing babies**?" (Matt 21:16)

Surprisingly, John indicates that the disciples did not grasp fully the significance of the moment (John 12:16). The Pharisees were utterly disgusted and said to one another, "Look, the world has gone after him" (v. 19). As John often does, he follows a significant event with a lengthy discourse (vv. 20–36). The main point is that Jesus's hour of glorification had arrived. He would be "lifted up," and God would draw all people to him. Jesus returned to Bethany at the end of the day.

Final Reflections

We can hardly imagine what this moment must have meant to Jesus. For approximately three years of ministry, he kept his identity quiet. He acknowledged his messianic identity to the Samaritan woman (John 4:25–26) and received Peter's confession at Caesarea Philippi (Mark 8:29). But he silenced the demons and refused to allow them to acknowledge his identity. He often told those he healed to say nothing about it. Now, at the culmination of his ministry, he declared himself to be Israel's King by riding into Jerusalem on the back of a donkey.

The responses to Jesus varied, much as they did throughout his ministry. Some in the crowd welcomed him as the prophet from Galilee. Others appear to have seen him clearly as Messiah, the King of Israel, and the Son of David. They most certainly did not understand that his messiahship involved his crucifixion. The religious leaders saw him as a problem. Those who knew the Scriptures best, and especially the messianic prophecies, failed to accept Jesus and rejected him as a fraud, a phony. Despite his miracles they saw only the demise of their own popularity with the crowds.

For Jesus, this event fulfilled Israel's sacred scriptures, especially Zechariah 9:9. Jesus went to great lengths to secure for himself a donkey to enter the city. Jerusalem was the city of the great King and the location of Israel's most sacred site, the temple. The celebration of the triumphal entry was somewhat muted when Jesus paused on the western slope of the Mount of Olives and wept over Jerusalem's future destruction. Jesus did not go through life emotionless or in some robotic fashion. He had a heart for people. All those emotions welled up within him as he looked at the city from the Mount of Olives.

We should ask ourselves how often we are overcome with emotion when we consider that many people we love and care about are on the precipice of God's judgment. I fear we sometimes get used to loved ones and friends not knowing Jesus. We need to shed more tears and pray more passionate prayers for their salvation.

Hymn of Response

Tell me the story of Jesus,
Write on my heart ev'ry word;
Tell me the story most precious,

Sweetest that ever was heard.
Tell how the angels, in chorus,
Sang as they welcomed His birth,
"Glory to God in the highest!
Peace and good tidings to earth."

Tell me the story of Jesus,
Write on my heart ev'ry word;
Tell me the story most precious,
Sweetest that ever was heard.

Fasting alone in the desert,
Tell of the days that are past;
How for our sins He was tempted,
Yet was triumphant at last.
Tell of the years of His labor,
Tell of the sorrow He bore;
He was despised and afflicted,
Homeless, rejected, and poor.

Tell me the story of Jesus,
Write on my heart every word;
Tell me the story most precious,
Sweetest that ever was heard.

Tell of the cross where they nailed Him,
Writhing in anguish and pain;
Tell of the grave where they laid Him,
Tell how He liveth again.
Love in that story so tender,
Clearer than ever I see:
Stay, let me weep while you whisper,
Love paid the ransom for me.

Tell me the story of Jesus,
Write on my heart every word;
Tell me the story most precious,
Sweetest that ever was heard.[18]

---

[18] Fanny Crosby, "Tell Me the Story of Jesus," 1880, *Baptist Hymnal*, #220.

CHAPTER 2

THE CURSING OF THE FIG TREE AND CLEARING OF THE TEMPLE

MONDAY: APRIL 3, AD 30

At Jesus's triumphal entry, he declared openly his messianic identity. The two major events on Monday—the cursing of the fig tree and the clearing of the temple—are prophetic acts that dramatically announced the coming destruction of Jerusalem and the temple. John does not describe these events but moves from Palm Sunday to the events in the upper room on Thursday night. Luke does not describe the cursing of the fig tree. The likely reason for Luke's omission is that he recounts Jesus telling a parable in 13:6–9 that makes a similar point.

The Cursing of the Fig Tree[1]

The cursing of the fig tree and the clearing of the temple both took place on Monday, while the discovery of the withered fig tree took place on Tuesday morning. Only Matthew and Mark record this incident. Matthew telescopes the event so that the tree withers "at once" (Matt 21:19). Mark offers a more chronological approach than Matthew, describing the discovery of the withered fig tree the morning following the cursing. Mark's arrangement of these events helps the reader better understand the theological connection between the fig tree and the temple. The cursing of the fig interprets the temple clearing as foreshadowing the future destruction of the temple. Mark intertwines the two events, revealing their connectedness. His A/B/A pattern is commonly known as a "Markan sandwich": (A) the cursing of the fig tree (Mark 11:14); (B) the clearing of the temple (vv. 15–17); and (A) the discovery of the withered fig tree (v. 21).

Jesus's hunger provided the opportunity for the second symbolic act of the week. Fig trees typically sprout leaves in March and begin to develop a green fig around the same time.[2] Mark's comment, "It was not the season for figs" (v. 13), helps the reader understand that Jesus's action was symbolic, since he would not expect to find edible figs at this time. Figs were not harvested until later in the spring. Jesus's action portended what was about to take place at the temple. Mark notes specifically that the disciples were listening when Jesus "cursed" the tree (v. 14). This event should not be understood as Jesus losing his temper, but as a prophetic act.

---

[1] Matt 21:18–22; Mark 11:12–14, 20–25.
[2] Schnabel, *Jesus in Jerusalem*, 166 (see chap. 1, n. 10).

The Old Testament uses fruitless fig trees in prophetic texts as symbols of judgment.

> All the stars in the sky will dissolve.
> The sky will roll up like a scroll,
> and its stars will all wither
> as leaves wither on the vine,
> and foliage on the fig tree. (Isa 34:4)

> "I will gather them and bring them to an end."
>   This is the LORD's declaration.
> "There will be no grapes on the vine,
> no figs on the fig tree,
> and even the leaf will wither.
> Whatever I have given them will be lost to them." (Jer 8:13)

The "cursing" of the fig tree points to the temple's destruction, for its failure to bear spiritual fruit to God's glory.[3] Fruitfulness was a part of Israel's covenant responsibility to God, and she had failed to bear fruit. Hosea 9:10 reads:

> I discovered Israel
> like grapes in the wilderness.
> I saw your ancestors
> like the first fruit of the fig tree in its first season.
> But they went to Baal-peor,
> consecrated themselves to Shame,

---

[3] Against this interpretation, see Schnabel, *Jesus in Jerusalem*, 167–68 (see chap. 1, n. 10). Schnabel argues against this reading based on the lack of parallels between the quoted Old Testament passages and the Gospel accounts of the story. Instead, he understands the main point of the cursing of the fig tree and clearing of the temple to be Jesus's teaching on the power of faith in prayer.

and became abhorrent,
like the thing they loved.

God expects his people to bear fruit for his glory. Of course, not all of Israel should be lumped in with the Jerusalem leadership; many—like Joseph and Mary, Zechariah and Elizabeth, Simeon, and Anna—longed for the coming of God's Messiah and lived righteous and devout lives. When Jesus arrived at the temple, he would not find the fruit God desired.[4]

The Temple Clearing[5]

The temple of Jerusalem in Jesus's day was one of the largest and most magnificent temples in the ancient world.[6] It occupied an area of more than 170,000 square yards. The Kidron Valley bordered the temple to the east and Tyropoeon Valley to the west. The old city of David was located south of the temple and the Antonia Fortress to the north. The temple of Jesus's day was the result of continual work and alteration started during the reign of Herod the Great, beginning in 20 BC. Herod's massive expansion and remodeling caused many to consider it to be

---

[4] W. D. Davies and Dale C. Allison Jr. believe the focus to be primarily on the leadership of Jerusalem and the temple. Davies and Allison, *A Critical and Exegetical Commentary on the Gospel According to Saint Matthew*, (London: T&T Clark, 1997), 3:151–52. Blomberg understands the fig tree to represent all of Israel. Craig L. Blomberg, *Matthew*, The New American Commentary, vol. 22 (Nashville: B&H, 1992), 318.

[5] Matt 21:12–13; Mark 11:15–19; Luke 19:45–48.

[6] On the temple, see Daniel M. Gurtner and Nicholas Perrin, "Temple," in Green, *Dictionary of Jesus and the Gospels*, 2nd ed., 939–47 (see chap. 1, n. 2). On the temple clearing, see Jostein Adna, "Temple Act," in Green, *Dictionary of Jesus and the Gospels*, 2nd ed., 947–52 (see chap. 1, n. 2).

Israel's third temple. The first temple was built by Solomon and destroyed by the Babylonians in 587 BC. The second temple was built by Zerubbabel and the returning exiles in 538 BC. The work begun by Herod the Great continued after his death and was not completed until shortly before its destruction in AD 70. The buildings were constructed from white limestone and glistened in the sunlight. One can only imagine how the bright Palestinian sun, beating down on the white limestone, would cause the buildings to glisten in the eyes of those looking on from a distance.

As Jesus entered Jerusalem through the eastern gate that morning, he knew exactly what he intended to do. The previous day he looked around the temple precinct and saw the commercialization taking place there. Jesus's temple clearing directly challenged the temple leadership's authority. His actions caused them to seek his destruction (Mark 11:18). In other words, Jesus must die (John 11:53). His popularity, however, was the major obstacle to their murderous plot. They would need to find an opportunity to arrest him apart from the crowds.

John describes a similar event at the beginning of Jesus's ministry (John 2:13–22). Scholars debate whether Jesus cleared the temple once or twice. Most scholars seem to hold to the opinion that Jesus did this only once, at the conclusion of his ministry. The thought would then be that John moved it forward for theological purposes. Scholars' primary arguments for holding to only one cleansing is that it does not seem likely that Jesus could have gotten away with it a second time. Surely, the religious leaders would be prepared for him and not allow him to do it again. The other reason for understanding the temple clearing to have happened only once is the fact that the two accounts are so similar in their descriptions.

I think that Jesus likely cleared the temple twice—once at the beginning of his messianic ministry and the other at the conclusion. The similarity of description is the result of similar events in the same place. We know from John's Gospel that Jesus made numerous trips to Jerusalem during his ministry, and over a period of a few years the leadership may very well have let down their guard. Finally, since it does not appear that the Romans got involved in the event, the temple clearings were likely performed on a smaller scale than often thought.

Jesus's actions took place in the Court of the Gentiles. While some may question whether the commercialization was his primary motivation, his words seem to suggest differently. The commercialization taking place there reflects a deeper issue—a lack of concern for the proper worship of God. While Jesus's action of clearing the temple is certainly prophetic in nature, a kingly element may be present as well. Earlier cleansings of the temple were performed by kings Josiah and Hezekiah, and Judas Maccabeus.[7]

Jesus expressed righteous indignation as he disrupted those who were buying and selling and overturned the money changers' tables. Traveling from distant lands with animals suitable for sacrifice would hardly be possible. Yet selling animals in the Court of the Gentiles was inappropriate, not to mention the seemingly exorbitant prices being charged.[8] Jesus's clearing of the temple is reminiscent of Jeremiah's diatribe against the temple.

---

[7] See 2 Kgs 23:1–7; 2 Chr 29:3–11; *1 Macc 4*; *2 Macc 10*.

[8] R. T. France, *The Gospel of Mark*, New International Greek Testament Commentary (Grand Rapids, MI: Eerdmans, 2002), 444.

"As for you, do not pray for these people. Do not offer a cry or a prayer on their behalf, and do not beg me, for I will not listen to you. Don't you see how they behave in the cities of Judah and in the streets of Jerusalem? The sons gather wood, the fathers light the fire, and the women knead dough to make cakes for the queen of heaven, and they pour out drink offerings to other gods so that they provoke me to anger. But are they really provoking me?" This is the LORD's declaration. "Isn't it they themselves being provoked to disgrace?"

Therefore, this is what the Lord GOD says: "Look, my anger—my burning wrath—is about to be poured out on this place, on people and animals, on the tree of the field, and on the produce of the land. My wrath will burn and not be quenched." (Jer 7:16–20)

The Jewish people were required to pay a half-shekel temple tax annually for the work of the temple (Exod 30:11–16). Pilgrims had to exchange their local coinage for Tyrian coins because of the purity of the silver of the coins. This exchange opened the door for charging exorbitant rates. Furthermore, people apparently used the temple courts as a shortcut through the city, demonstrating a disregard for the temple's sacredness (Mark 11:16). Jesus condemned these practices because the Court of the Gentiles—which should have been "a house of prayer for all nations" (v. 17)—had turned into a place of merchandising and a thoroughfare. Jesus's reference, "for all nations," comes from Isa 56:7:

I will bring them to my holy mountain
and let them rejoice in my house of prayer.
Their burnt offerings and sacrifices
will be acceptable on my altar,

for my house will be called a house of prayer
for all nations.

The context of this passage in Isaiah is part of the prophet's emphasis on the procession of the nations to Zion, the promise that in the Messianic Age all peoples of the earth would come and worship in the temple. The commercialism in the temple demeaned its very purpose. King Solomon looked forward to a day when all nations would worship at the temple.

Even for the foreigner who is not of your people Israel
but has come from a distant land
because of your name—
for they will hear of your great name,
strong hand, and outstretched arm,
and will come and pray toward this temple—
may you hear in heaven, your dwelling place,
and do according to all the foreigner asks.
Then all peoples of earth will know your name,
to fear you as your people Israel do
and to know that this temple I have built
bears your name. (1 Kgs 8:41–43)

In Mark 11:17 Jesus deliberately contrasted "house of prayer" with "den of thieves" when he quoted Jer 7:11:

Has this house, which bears my name, become a den of robbers in your view? Yes, I too have seen it.
This is the LORD's declaration.

In the context, Jeremiah condemned the apostate nation for robbery, murder, immorality, idolatry, and for turning God's house into "a den of robbers." The unscrupulous motives of the leaders had brought down God's judgment upon his people. As a result of Jesus's actions and words, the religious leaders began looking for a way to kill him. However, they feared him because of his popularity with the crowds. When evening came, Jesus departed the city to return to Bethany (Mark 11:19).

The Discovery of the Withered Fig Tree[9]

Technically, the discovery of the withered fig tree happened on Tuesday morning, but I will discuss it here because of its connection to the cursing of the fig tree and the clearing of the temple. On the way into Jerusalem on Tuesday morning, the disciples discovered that the fig tree that Jesus cursed had withered (Mark 11:20). Jesus used the discovery as an opportunity to teach his disciples on the topics of prayer, faith, and forgiveness. His point was that God does great things in response to the prayers of his people. Speaking hyperbolically to emphasize his point, Jesus told them that when God's people pray, he can move mountains in response (Matt 21:21; Mark 11:23–24). When God's people pray, however, they must not harbor bitterness toward others. Bitterness and unforgiveness are detrimental to prayer. Faith is demonstrated in both praying to God and forgiving others (Mark 11:25).

Final Reflections

Jesus cursed the fig tree and cleared the temple to demonstrate that Jerusalem would be judged for its fruitlessness. When Jesus examined the temple, which stood at the very heart of Judaism,

---

[9] Matt 21:18–21; Mark 11:20–25.

he found it wanting. It had all the beauty of a place set aside for God's glory, but under the beautiful façade of prayer and sacrifice lived a den of robbers. The religious leadership turned the temple into a commercial bazaar for personal financial gain. When Gentiles prayed to God, they would have to battle the smell of animals, the stench of animal dung, the bleating of sheep, and the clamoring of the money changers. We can only imagine how this must have caused Jesus's holy blood to boil in righteous indignation.

Paul warned Timothy about those who use religion simply for gain (1 Tim 6:3–5). What was true in the first century is no less true in the twenty-first century. Some ministries on television and radio have become nothing more than religious marketplaces for the buying and selling of religious "helps." They marginalize the teaching of the Word of God for the profiteering of the so-called minister. The same is true in some Christian organizations where the leaders tend to live more like Fortune-500 CEOs than godly servant-leaders. A similar attitude exists in many who sit in the pews, who are more enamored with their retirement portfolios than living for God's honor. Materialism and consumerism make up two of Satan's biggest traps for Western Christianity.

Hymn of Response

One awful word which Jesus spoke,
Against the tree which bore no fruit;
More piercing than the lightning's stroke,
Blasted and dried it to the root.

But could a tree the Lord offend,
To make him show his anger thus?
He surely had a farther end,

To be a warning word to us.

The fig tree by its leaves was known,
But having not a fig to show;
It brought a heavy sentence down,
Let none hereafter on thee grow.

Too many, who the Gospel hear,
Whom Satan blinds and sin deceives;
We to this fig tree may compare,
They yield no fruit, but only leaves.

Knowledge, and zeal, and gifts, and talk,
Unless combined with faith and love,
And witnessed.by a Gospel walk,
Will not a true profession prove.

Without the fruit the Lord expects
Knowledge will make our state the worse;
The barren tree He still rejects,
And soon will blast them with His curse.

O Lord, unite our hearts in prayer!
On each of us Thy Spirit send;
That we the fruits of grace may bear,
And find acceptance in the end.[10]

---

[10] John Newton, "One Awful Word Which Jesus Spoke," 1779, *The Cyber Hymnal*, #8750, Hymnary.org, https://hymnary.org/hymn/CYBER/8750.

CHAPTER 3

TEMPLE CONTROVERSIES AND TEACHING

TUESDAY: APRIL 4, AD 30

When Jesus arrived in the city on Tuesday morning, he was confronted by a series of hostile questions that were intended to trap him in front of the crowds. Jesus's battle of wits with his opponents demonstrates his wisdom and incredibly deep understanding of the Scriptures. The first four questions came from Jesus's opponents, but he turned the table on them and asked a final question they were unable to answer. He condemned the hypocritical leadership and commended an impoverished widow. After leaving the city and sitting on the Mount of Olives, Jesus predicted Jerusalem's destruction and his second coming. What a day!

The Withered Fig Tree

As mentioned in chapter 2, while Jesus and the disciples were making their way into Jerusalem on Tuesday morning, the disciples discovered that the fig tree Jesus cursed had withered. Jesus used it as an opportunity to teach them on the topics of prayer, faith, and forgiveness. His point was that God does great things in response to the prayers of his people.

Temple Controversies[1]

The temple courts became a theological battleground between Jesus and his enemies. At every turn Jesus demonstrated the depth of his wisdom. The first question focuses attention on the previous day's disturbance in the temple.

Question 1: "By what authority are you doing these things?"[2]

As mentioned above, the first question came from the leading priests, scribes, and elders and related to the previous day's clearing of the temple. This group was representative of the Sanhedrin, the Jewish ruling council. They wanted to know who gave Jesus authority to clear the temple. Jesus responded by asking them a question concerning the origin of John's baptism—was it from God or humans? The implicit point is that both John's baptism and Jesus's authority came from God. The inquisitors were not put off by Jesus's responding with a question, which was a rather typical form of argumentation among the teachers of the day.

As Jesus's opponents conferred, they realized that he had backed them into a corner. The people believed John to be a prophet from God. If they were to say his baptism was from

---

[1] Matt 21:23–23:39; Mark 11:27–12:40; Luke 20:1–47.
[2] Matt 21:23–22:14; Mark 11:27–12:12; Luke 20:1–19.

humans, then the crowds would stone them; but if they said it was from God, then they would be asked why they refused to be baptized by John. Since they did not answer Jesus's question, he refused to answer theirs.

Jesus responded to the leaders by asking another question: "What do you think?" He went on to tell three parables.[3] In the first parable Jesus drew a contrast between two sons (Matt 21:28–32). The father in the story approached the first son and asked him to go to work in the vineyard. The son initially refused to go, but afterward he regretted his decision and went to work in the field. The father went to the second son and asked him to go work in the field. The second son agreed to go, but then did not. Jesus asked the penetrating question, "Which of the two did his father's will?" (v. 31). Jesus's opponents unwittingly responded, "The first." The obvious point of the parable is that the first son represents the "tax collectors and prostitutes," who were entering the kingdom of God rather than those interrogating Jesus. The former responded to John the Baptist's call to repentance, while the latter group did not.

Jesus's second parable is a further condemnation of the religious leaders (Matt 21:33–46; Mark 12:1–12; Luke 20:9–19). The parable of the Vineyard Owner demonstrates both God's patience and judgment. The background to this parable is the "Song of the Vineyard" in Isa 5:1–7. The imagery would have been familiar to Jesus's audience: a landowner plants a vineyard, builds a lookout tower, puts a fence around the vineyard, and digs a pit for a wine vat. Jesus's audience would have understood the story as an allegory condemning the Jewish leadership.

---

[3] Matthew records all three parables while Mark and Luke record only the second of the three.

The main points are evident: the vineyard represents Israel; the tenants represent Israel's leaders; the owner represents God; and the servants represent the Old Testament prophets (Amos 3:7; Zech 1:6). Throughout Israel's history they rejected God's prophets (1 Kgs 18:13; 19:10, 14; Jer 26:20–23; Neh 9:26). The beloved son represents Jesus, and the murder of the son represents Jesus's death. The giving of the vineyard to others represents the judgment coming upon Israel and the establishment of the church. The interpretation of the death of the son would have been more understandable to the readers of the Gospels than the original audience, but the religious leaders understood clearly enough, and they sought to arrest Jesus. God's patience is demonstrated in the parable by the continual sending of prophets despite Israel's failure to heed their warnings.

The parable concludes with two rhetorical questions. The first is, "What then will the owner of the vineyard do?" (Mark 12:9). The owner of the vineyard is none other than God himself. Those who thought they controlled the vineyard find themselves cast out and the vineyard given to others. The second rhetorical question leads to Jesus's quote of Psalm 118:22–23:

"Haven't you read this Scripture:

> **The stone that the builders rejected**
> **has become the cornerstone.**
> **This came about from the Lord**
> **and is wonderful in our eyes?"** (Mark 12:10–11)

The rejected stone is the rejected Son. Psalm 118 is a thanksgiving hymn that celebrates David's victory over his enemies and was quoted at Jesus's triumphal entry. David was a cornerstone—rejected but ultimately victorious. Jesus is the greater David—rejected by his countrymen but nonetheless the cornerstone.[4] Matthew adds Jesus's words, "The kingdom of God will be taken away from you and given to a people producing its fruit" (Matt 21:43). The religious leaders knew he spoke the parable against them. They wanted to arrest him but failed to act because they were cowards. They would wait until they were under the cover of darkness and the crowds were absent. God's judgment would come through the invasion of the Roman army.

Jesus's next parable concerns God's great wedding banquet (Matt 22:1–14). The parable unfolds in three scenes. In the first scene the king sent out his servants to call those who had been invited. But they refused to come. The king was concerned that they should come, and again sent out other servants with a more urgent call requesting their presence. But they still refused. The king was furious and sent troops to put to death those who rejected his gracious invitation.

In the second scene of the parable, the king sent his servants out into the highways and byways to bring as many as would come (both evil and good) to the joyous festivities. Finally, the wedding hall was filled with guests. The third and final scene of the parable details the discovery of an intruder to the feast. This intruder was not dressed appropriately. The clothing represents the righteous character of those attending the feast. Rejection of the stipulated wedding garment indicates a disregard and disloyalty toward the host of the feast. The kingdom of God demands in its subjects both a proper confession of faith and a lifestyle that is commensurate with that confession. The intruder without the appropriate clothing was cast "into the outer darkness, where there will be weeping and gnashing of teeth" (Matt 22:13).

---

[4] See Acts 4:11; 1 Pet 2:4, 6–7.

Question 2: "Is it lawful to pay taxes to Caesar, or not?"[5]

Having failed in challenging Jesus's authority, his opponents tried to alienate him from the crowd. The presence of the Herodians with the Pharisees is odd, since they were not allies and disagreed on most issues. The Herodians were supporters of the Herodian dynasty installed by Rome as client-kings. The Herodians were very political, while the Pharisees were much less political. The two groups began by flattering Jesus. The four insincere compliments describe Jesus's integrity, fairness, impartiality, and truthfulness. The irony is that what they did not truly believe about Jesus was true of him. Obviously, they were hoping to catch him off guard by their flattery.

They questioned him about paying the poll-tax. This tax was to be paid by all adults living in Judea under Roman rule. As a Galilean, Jesus was not responsible for paying the tax. The amount of the annual tax was one denarius, which was equal to one day's wage for a common laborer. This tax was a very volatile issue in Judea, and Jesus was fully aware of their duplicity. They believed they had Jesus between a rock and a hard place. If he answered yes, then the crowds would be upset with him; and if he answered no, then he would put himself in opposition to the Roman government.

Jesus responded by requesting that he be given a denarius, the very amount of the tax. The coin had Emperor Tiberius's image on it.[6] The coin also included the inscriptions, "Tiberius Caesar Augustus, son of [the] divine Augustus" on the one side and "high priest" on the other. The image on the coin was idolatrous and

---

[5] Matt 22:15–22; Mark 12:13–17; Luke 20:20–26.
[6] Emperor Tiberius reigned AD 14–37.

the inscriptions blasphemous. How interesting that those asking the question were the ones who had the coin while Jesus did not. Jesus's response was brilliant! "Give to Caesar the things that are Caesar's, and to God the things that are God's" (Mark 12:17). His words cannot be taken as those of an anti-Roman zealot in opposition to Jewish taxation by Caesar. However, Jesus's statement cannot be understood as pro-Roman either, because service to God is fundamental, and God was ultimately over Caesar.[7]

Question 3: "In the resurrection . . . whose wife will she be?"[8]

The next question put to Jesus concerns the resurrection of the dead. The Sadducees were a priestly group and dominated the Sanhedrin. They did not believe in a future bodily resurrection from the dead. The scenario they presented to Jesus is a ridiculous application of the Old Testament law of levirate marriage (Deut 25:5–10). According to Old Testament law, when a man died without an heir, his brother was to marry the widow and produce children to carry on the family line. The first son of this marriage was considered to be the son of the dead brother. The Sadducees' purpose was to show the supposedly ridiculous concept of a future bodily resurrection from the dead.

Jesus pointed out two errors in the Sadducees' thinking. First, he rebuked them because of their ignorance of the Scriptures. The Sadducees would have been insulted greatly by Jesus's rebuke, since they were well educated in the Scriptures. The resurrection

---

[7] See Rom 13:1–7 and 1 Pet 2:13–17 for further insight on the relationship between Christians and government.

[8] Matt 22:23–33; Mark 12:18–27; Luke 20:27–40.

of the dead is referred to most clearly in the Old Testament Prophets and Writings.[9] However, the Sadducees accepted only the Torah (Genesis–Deuteronomy) as the ultimate authority, so Jesus answered them from the Torah. He pointed to Moses's encounter with God at the burning bush (Exod 3:6, 15–16) and demonstrated that God's covenant with the patriarchs did not end at their deaths. They are still alive, for God is the God of the living and not the dead. God's covenant relationship with his people extends beyond their physical death, which means that the afterlife must be a reality.

Second, Jesus challenged the Sadducees' failure to understand God's power. They assumed that the age to come would be an extension of the present age, which is not true. God can give bodies suitable for the present age, and he can also give bodies suitable for an eternal age (see 1 Cor 15:20–58). In this new existence there is no need for sexual reproduction because there is no more death. Intimacy and marriage are superseded by fellowship of a multitude of fellow believers with one another, and especially with God. In this sense believers will be like the angels (Matt 22:30).

Question 4: "Which command is the most important of all?"[10]

A scribe, who overheard Jesus's answer and recognized his wisdom, asked him, "Which command is the most important

---

[9] For references on the resurrection of the dead in the Old Testament, see Job 19:26; Pss 16:9–11; 49:15; 73:25–26; Isa 26:19; Ezek 37:1–14; and Dan 12:2.

[10] Matt 22:34–40; Mark 12:28–34. Luke likely did not record this question since it was asked earlier in his Gospel in 10:25–37.

of all?" (Mark 12:28). The Law contained 613 separate commands, and Jewish leaders frequently argued about which of them were more important than others. While no commandment of God is unimportant, some were recognized as more significant than others.

Jesus's reply combines two commands from the Law. The first, Deuteronomy 6:4–5, is known as the Shema because it begins with the Hebrew word translated "listen" (*shema*). The greatest commandment corresponds to the first part of the Ten Commandments (Exod 20:2–11), which deals with a person's relationship to God. The oneness of God is foundational to Jewish and Christian monotheism and is the basis for the command to love God with wholehearted devotion.

The second great command is from Leviticus 19:18. This commandment corresponds to the second part of the Ten Commandments (Exod 20:12–17), which concerns a person's relationship with others. The words "as yourself" mean to love others just as much as you love yourself. This love, however, is not a call to some sort of self-centered love. Jesus taught his disciples that they should be the "servant[s] of all" (Mark 9:35; 10:43–44). The point is that everyone cares for themselves and their physical and emotional well-being. We should love others with the same intentionality we extend to ourselves.[11]

The two commands are not independent of each other but are intricately related as one command. Their integration precludes a spiritual life that is concerned only with one's own spiritual growth on the one hand and, on the other hand,

---

[11] The frequent repetition of the command to love others emphasizes its importance to the early church (Matt 5:43–44; 19:19; 25:31–46; Rom 13:8–10; Gal 5:14; Jas 2:8).

unconcerned with serving others. God demands that we be serious about our relationship with him, and that relationship is to be worked out in serving others. The scribe's response—that loving God and neighbor is more important than all offerings and sacrifices—emphasizes the foundational nature of these two commandments.

Question 5: "How can the scribes say that the Messiah is the son of David?"[12]

The previous passage concluded, "And no one dared to question him any longer" (Mark 12:34). In verse 35 Jesus asked a rhetorical question that delighted the crowd: "How can the scribes say the Messiah is the son of David?" He answered the question by referring to Psalm 110:1.[13] His answer confirms Davidic authorship of the psalm and attributes David's words to the inspiration of the Holy Spirit.

Jesus then asked the logical question: "David himself calls him 'Lord.' How, then, can he be his son?" Psalm 110:1 is the most frequently quoted Old Testament verse in the New Testament and was also read in the past at the coronation of Israel's kings. Jesus's quote was not a denial that he is the Davidic Messiah but an affirmation that he is more than the Davidic Messiah—he is a descendant of David and, at the same time, David's God.[14] Jesus's being seated at God's right hand is a way of stating he is in the

---

[12] Matt 22:41–46; Mark 12:35–37; Luke 20:41–44.

[13] Psalm 110 becomes the dominant proof-text for the exaltation of Jesus in the early church. See Acts 2:33–36; Rom 8:34; 1 Cor 15:25; Col 3:1; and Heb 1:3, 13.

[14] See 2 Sam 7:12–13. When the Davidic dynasty ceased to rule, toward the end of the divided monarchy, the covenant promise centered on

position of power and glory. It is an acknowledgment he will be victorious over his enemies, even though at that moment things looked ominous.

Condemnation of the Pharisees and Scribes[15]

Jesus turned his attention to the Pharisees and scribes, his harshest critics. This passage has often been accused of being anti-Semitic. The accusation seems to ignore the fact that Matthew and Mark, who recorded Jesus's words, were both Jewish (Luke was a Gentile). Furthermore, the one who spoke these words was himself Jewish. Jesus's words are no sterner than the condemnation of Israel by the Old Testament prophets; nor were Jesus's words directed against all Jewish people. The New Testament extols the virtues of many faithful Jewish people—Simeon and Anna, Joseph and Mary, Zechariah and Elizabeth—and the list could go on. In Matthew's account Jesus's final words are an expression of deep grief over the nation's spiritual condition (Matt 23:37–39). Those are hardly the words of someone who is anti-Semitic!

Matthew's account of this strong denunciation is much longer (thirty-six verses) than Mark's and Luke's accounts (three verses). The probable reason is that Matthew's intended audience needed to "hear" more of what Jesus thought about the current Jewish leadership in Jerusalem. Each evangelist gives enough information to communicate Jesus's abhorrence of the religious hypocrisy.

---

a coming one, labeling that person the righteous branch of David. Also see Isa 11:1 and Jer 23:5–6.

[15] Matt 23:1–39; Mark 12:38–40; Luke 20:45–47.

Mark's summary of Jesus's words highlights three major charges against the scribes (Mark 12:38–40). First, they were selfishly ambitious. They looked for honor from men rather than from God, which is why they walked around in long robes and yearned for respectful greetings in the marketplaces. Second, they were arrogant. They loved the best seats and sought to sit at tables with the most prominent people. Whether in a religious setting, or a secular one, they always wanted pride of place with the most important people. Jesus's approach was so different. He came to minister and serve those who were on the fringes of society. Third, the scribes were greedy. They preyed on the most vulnerable, "devour[ing] widow's houses." With few words, Jesus laid bare their crooked hearts.

Matthew includes Jesus's lament over Jerusalem (Matt 23:37–39). Jesus's pronouncement of doom did not diminish his love for the city and her inhabitants. He wanted to protect them, like a hen protects her chicks, but their refusal to welcome him as Messiah sealed their doom. Verse 39 is a transition from the prophecy of judgment to a description of that judgment in the invasion by Rome in AD 70.

The Widow's Mite[16]

In the final moments before Jesus left the temple, he expressed to his disciples how impressed he was with an unnamed widow's offering. Jesus situated himself in a place (the Court of the Women) that allowed him to watch as people placed their offerings into the temple treasury. Jesus did not comment as he

---

[16] Mark 12:41–44; Luke 21:1–4. Matthew does not describe this incident.

watched the wealthy place large sums into the treasury; but after seeing a widow drop in two tiny coins that were worth very little, he called his disciples together for a teaching moment. Widows were some of the most vulnerable people in the ancient world. The two small coins were worth 1/64 of a denarius. So her offering would have barely been enough to buy a very modest amount of food for a single meal. The point is that from a worldly perspective her offering was inconsequential. The key lesson on giving learned from this impoverished lady is that one's giving is not measured by amount, but by sacrifice.

The widow's devotion to God is contrasted with the Pharisees and scribes by its placement in Mark and Luke. Earlier in Jesus's ministry he watched the rich young ruler turn and walk away from him because he was unwilling to sacrifice everything to follow Jesus. Here, we read about a widow who found the pearl of great value and gave her all to obtain that finest of pearls (Matt 13:45–46). Those who give all to follow Jesus will find in him all they need and could ever want! Blessed be the name of the Lord for the example of this widow.

The Olivet Discourse[17]

The Olivet Discourse is also known as Jesus's Eschatological Discourse. The discourse is recorded in each of the Synoptic Gospels. Matthew's account is significantly longer than Mark's and Luke's accounts. The interpretation of the discourse is complex, and scholars debate its exact meaning. The issue is determining when Jesus addressed the events surrounding the destruction of Jerusalem and when he addressed his second coming. As for

---

[17] Matt 24:1–25:46; Mark 13:1–37; Luke 21:5–36.

the destruction of the temple, Jesus had addressed it throughout the week: the cursing of the fruitless fig tree; the clearing of the temple; Jesus's harsh condemnation of the religious leaders depicted in the parable of the Vineyard Owner; and his stern rebuke of the Pharisees and scribes. Jesus made it abundantly clear that divine judgment was coming. The disciples may have thought the destruction of temple and Christ's second coming would happen simultaneously.[18]

I understand Jesus to be answering both questions. Some aspects of the discourse focus on the destruction of Jerusalem and others on Jesus's second coming. At certain points the events surrounding Jerusalem's fall in AD 70 foreshadow events at Jesus's second coming.[19]

The following chart provides an overview of the discourse.

---

[18] There are essentially three approaches to the discourse, with slight variations within each. The preterist approach understands most, if not all, of the discourse to refer to the destruction of Jerusalem in AD 70. The partial preterist view understands Matt 24:1–35 (and the parallels in Mark and Luke) to refer to the destruction of Jerusalem and only Matt 24:36–51 (and parallels) to Christ's return. For this view, see R. T. France, *Matthew*, Tyndale New Testament Commentaries (Leicester: InterVarsity, 1985), 333. At the opposite extreme is traditional dispensationalism, which understands the entire discourse to refer to Jesus's return. For this view, see John F. Walvoord, *Matthew: Thy Kingdom Come* (Chicago: Moody, 1974). For a progressive dispensational approach, see Darrell L. Bock, *Jesus according to Scripture: Restoring the Portrait from the Gospels* (Grand Rapids, MI: Baker Academic, 2002), 338–554.

[19] I have been influenced to varying degrees by George R. Beasley-Murray, *Jesus and the Last Days: The Interpretation of the Olivet Discourse* (Peabody, MA: Hendrickson, 1993); Craig L. Blomberg, *Matthew*, The New American Commentary (see chap. 2, n. 4); D. A. Carson, *Matthew*, The Expositor's Bible Commentary, ed. Tremper Longman III and David E. Garland (Grand Rapids, MI: Zondervan, 2017).

JESUS'S OLIVET DISCOURSE

The Setting
Matt 24:1–3; Mark 13:1;
Luke 21:5–7

Beginning of Birth Pains
Matt 24:4–14; Mark 13:5–13;
Luke 21:8–19

Destruction of Jerusalem
Matt 24:13–28; Mark 13:14–23;
Luke 21:20–24

Coming of the Son of Man
Matt 24:29–31; Mark 13:24–27;
Luke 21:25–28

Parable of the Fig Tree
Matt 24:45–51

Importance of Vigilance
Matt 24:42–44; Mark 13:33–37;
Luke 21:34–36

Parable of the Servant
Matt 24:45–51

Parable of the Ten Vigins
Matt 25:14–30

Parable of the Talents
Matt 25:14–30

Parable of the Sheep and the Goats
Matt 25:31–46

The Setting for the Discourse[20]

After spending a day in theological debate with the religious leaders, Jesus left the temple for the short walk back to Bethany. Even though the disciples had seen the temple many times, they were still astonished by its beauty and grandeur. Jesus's response to their comment concerning the temple must have stunned them: "Do you see these great buildings? Not one stone will be left upon another—all will be thrown down" (Mark 13:2). The Jerusalem temple was the largest temple complex in the ancient world. With its white stones, gold trim, and gold-covered roof, the temple complex glistened in the sunlight. Jesus and his disciples would have exited the city through the Eastern Gate, crossed the Kidron Valley, and walked up the western slope of the Mount of Olives overlooking the city.

The Beginning of Birth Pains[21]

Jesus's first four followers (Peter, Andrew, James, and John) questioned him about his comments concerning the temple. Matthew makes it clear the disciples asked Jesus two questions: "Tell us, when will these things happen? And what is the sign of your coming and of the end of the age?" (Matt 24:3). The first question has to do with the destruction of the temple and the second with Jesus's second coming.

After the disciples questioned him concerning the timing of these events, Jesus made a helpful clarification, indicating there would be some preliminary events not signaling the immediate end—of either Jerusalem or the world. He warned them ("Watch

---

[20] Matt 24:1–3; Mark 13:1–4; Luke 21:5–7.
[21] Matt 24:4–14; Mark 13:5–13; Luke 21:8–19.

out") about the danger of deception; specifically, about people claiming to be the Messiah. He then listed a series of natural and moral disasters people often wrongly associate with the immediate end of the world. Jesus's use of the Greek term translated "must" (*dei*) indicates God's sovereignty over these events. He said, "It is not yet the end" and "These are the beginning of birth pains" (Mark 13:7–8). But just as birth pains precede childbirth, God's judgment will inevitably follow.

Jesus warned his disciples to be on guard concerning the coming persecution. He did not want them to be surprised when persecution came. This persecution would be both religious and governmental. We need only to read the book of Acts to see how quickly Jesus's words came to pass.[22] He then added, "It is necessary that the gospel be preached to all nations" (v. 10). Despite tremendous persecution, the gospel ("good news") would be proclaimed throughout the world and would take place before the destruction of Jerusalem. Paul understood the gospel to have been proclaimed throughout the world in his day.[23]

The disciples were encouraged to not be afraid when they experienced persecution. The Spirit would assist them in defending their faith. The world's hatred of Christianity would be so intense that family members would betray family members, even to the point of execution. Ultimately, the world's hatred was the result of its hatred toward Jesus, and they expressed it in their persecution of his people.[24] Although this hatred would be worldwide, those who endured to the end demonstrated their genuine faith in Christ.

---

[22] See Acts 4:1–22; 24:10–27; 25:1–26:32; 2 Cor 11:24–25.

[23] See Rom 16:26; Col 1:6, 23. For further study on these thoughts, see Rom 1:5, 8; 10:18; 15:19, 23.

[24] See John 15:18–16:4.

The Abomination of Desolation and Subsequent Events[25]

The central section of the discourse is quite difficult. I understand two things to be going on here. First, Jesus was describing the destruction of Jerusalem (answering the disciples' first question). Second, the devastating destruction of Jerusalem foreshadowed events at the end of human history (answering the disciples' second question). Therefore, the fall of Jerusalem and the destruction of the temple foreshadowed the final days of human history.

The phrase "abomination of desolation" has caused no small amount of controversy. The phrase is found three times in Daniel.

> He will make a firm covenant
> with many for one week,
> but in the middle of the week
> he will put a stop to sacrifice and offering.
> And the abomination of desolation
> will be on a wing of the temple
> until the decreed destruction
> is poured out on the desolator. (Dan 9:27)

> His forces will rise up and desecrate the temple fortress. They will abolish the regular sacrifice and set up the abomination of desolation. (Dan 11:31)

> From the time the daily sacrifice is abolished and the abomination of desolation is set up, there will be 1,290 days. (Dan 12:11)

---

[25] Matt 24:15–28; Mark 13:14–23; Luke 21:20–24.

The prophecies in Daniel point first to 167 BC, when the Syrian king, Antiochus Epiphanes, desecrated the temple by sacrificing a pig on the altar. Jesus's prophecy picks up on Daniel and points first to Titus's entry into the temple during the siege of Jerusalem in AD 70. Second, and finally, it points beyond that event to the final enemy of God, the Antichrist (2 Thess 2:1–11; Rev 13:1–8). Mark inserts a parenthetical warning to his readers to be wise and careful in reading this material (Mark 13:14). Good advice indeed!

Jesus provided five examples of the desperate situation that would take place in AD 70: (1) Those in the city should flee to the mountains; (2) No one should seek to collect their possessions before fleeing; (3) Those in the fields must not return to their homes; (4) Those days would be extremely difficult for pregnant women and those with young children; and (5) They should pray that these events do not take place in the winter when survival would be very difficult.[26] Luke makes it clear that these events related first to the fall of Jerusalem: "When you see Jerusalem surrounded by armies, then recognize that its desolation has come near" (Luke 21:20).

Jesus's language, however, was so intense that his words likely foreshadow a time beyond the fall of Jerusalem and to the final days of human history that will culminate in his return. If God does not cut short those days, no one will survive; but God will cut them short because of his elect. Just as in the days leading up to the fall of Jerusalem, in the final days God's people must be careful not to be deceived. Jesus spoke of deceptive signs and wonders.[27] Paul instructed the Thessalonian believers:

---

[26] Matt 24:15–20; Mark 13:14–18; Luke 21:20–23.
[27] Matt 24:21–28; Mark 13:19–23.

The coming of the lawless one is based on Satan's working, with every kind of miracle, both signs and wonders serving the lie, and with every wicked deception among those who are perishing. They perish because they did not accept the love of the truth and so be saved. For this reason, God sends them a strong delusion so that they will believe the lie, so that all will be condemned—those who did not believe the truth but delighted in unrighteousness. (2 Thess 2:9–12)

The Return of the Son of Man[28]

The Synoptic evangelists describe in brief words Christ's second coming. Jesus warned in Mark 13:24–25 that "after that tribulation" (the one just described) there will be signs of cosmic upheaval. These events should be contrasted with the earlier reference to natural upheavals of earthquakes and famines. Jesus quoted from Daniel to describe his glorious return (Dan 7:13–14). Jesus will descend from heaven and gather his people from one end of the earth to the other.

Signs of Nearness, but an Unknown Time[29]

Jesus then moved on from the events of the eschaton to the absolute necessity of vigilance on the part of his followers. He had spoken of the destruction of Jerusalem and the final days of human history, and now he would conclude his teaching on these topics. Jesus applied the parable of the fig tree to the present discussion.

---

[28] Matt 24:29–31; Mark 13:24–27; Luke 21:25–28.
[29] Matt 24:32–41; Mark 13:28–32; Luke 21:29–33.

As we have seen, Jesus combined the fall of Jerusalem with the foreshadowing of the great tribulation in the final days. If we are correct in seeing Jesus as intentionally blending these two events, then the same can likely be said of Mark 13:30 and its parallels: "Truly I tell you, this generation will certainly not pass away until all these things take place." The generation living during the ministry of Jesus would be alive when Jerusalem fell in AD 70; but beyond that, when the events of history begin to unfold in the final days, that generation will be alive for Jesus's return.

In a world destined for destruction, the disciples' only hope was to place their faith in God and his Word. Jesus referred to "my Words," which include all he said in the discourse, but even beyond that to all he taught his disciples (v. 31). Jesus's words are eternal; his teachings are more enduring than the fundamental elements of creation. The basic elements of creation will pass away, but Jesus's words will not.[30] Isaiah 51:6 reads:

Look up to the heavens,
and look at the earth beneath;
for the heavens will vanish like smoke,
the earth will wear out like a garment,
and its inhabitants will die like gnats.
But my salvation will last forever,
and my righteousness will never be shattered.

When we read "Now concerning that day or hour no one knows—neither the angels in heaven nor the Son—but only the Father" (Mark 13:32), we need to remember that Jesus was fully God and fully man. We should not forget that the main point Jesus was making is the importance of being ready. If the Son

---

[30] See Ps 102:26; 2 Pet 3:7, 10, 12.

himself did not know the day or hour, Christians should keep from seeking such knowledge for themselves.

Parables to Encourage Watchfulness[31]

Jesus told his disciples a series of parables to encourage vigilance and faithfulness. In some of these parables Jesus's return was sooner than expected; and in others, it was later than expected. Regardless of when he returns, his followers must be ready. Until that time, God's people are to remain busy serving him. Waiting on him does not encourage idleness, but service.

So, this turbulent Tuesday ends on an emotional note. Jesus predicted the destruction of Jerusalem and the end of the world. He spent a good part of the day in a series of confrontations with his enemies. At each turn, Jesus's wisdom and knowledge of Scripture confounded his opponents and humiliated them in front of the crowds. Jesus and the disciples then returned to Bethany for a much-needed rest.

Final Reflections

If the events discussed in this chapter all took place on Tuesday of Passion Week, then the day was quite full for Jesus. Between the discovery of the withered fig tree and his predictions of the destruction of the temple and the end of the world, Jesus battled his harshest critics. Of all that took place on that day, a few truths stand out for special comment.

First, Jesus hates religious hypocrisy. He made that clear the previous day by his clearing of the temple. He reiterated his

---

[31] Matt 24:42–25:30; Mark 13:33–37; Luke 21:34–36.

feelings on this day in his lengthy condemnation of the Pharisees and scribes. Jesus made it evident that why we serve is as important as how we serve. The Pharisees and scribes did many of the right things—prayer, participation in the sacrificial system, and the giving of alms—but they longed for the approval of men more than the approval of God. Most people begin their life of service to God for the right reasons, but over time some become enamored with the praise of people. Hypocrisy and pride blind some persons to their own sin and skew their perspective on godliness and kingdom service. Those whom Jesus condemned demonstrate that you can perform religious activities but not have a love for God. They failed to believe their own Scriptures:

> Does the LORD take pleasure in burnt offerings and
>   sacrifices
> as much as in obeying the LORD?
> Look: to obey is better than sacrifice,
> to pay attention is better than the fat of rams. (1 Sam 15:22)

Their knowledge of the Scriptures made them arrogant rather than more loving (1 Cor 8:1). The Pharisees and scribes are examples of the danger of religion without conversion.

Second, we learn from the impoverished widow that no good deed done for God's glory goes unnoticed by him. As far as she knew, no one was watching as she placed her two small coins into the temple treasury. Little did she know, the Son of God would use her as an illustration of genuine generosity and godliness. She was the exact opposite of the Pharisees and scribes. While they performed their "righteous acts" to be noticed by humans, she gave her gift expecting no recognition. We can live our lives for the recognition of others or for the glory of God. The former brings momentary notoriety and acclaim, but the latter an eternal blessing. This is wonderful news to the pastor who serves a small flock in a rural community with little hope of numerical growth. Jesus takes great pleasure in that pastor's ministry, although he may never speak at a denominational gathering. The same is true of the missionary serving on the foreign field who sows gospel seed in a very hard place with no noticeable results. God sees and knows.

Third, the most important truth Jesus taught on this day was about his second coming. Although the day and hour of his return are unknown, the reality of his coming is certain. Therefore, the church must be spiritually alert until that day. God's people should not spend their time trying to determine something they cannot know—when Jesus will return. Rather than speculating on the timing of his return, God's people must remain spiritually alert. Spiritual alertness involves serving God's people (doing the right thing) for God's glory (for the right reason). Then, whether his coming is sooner than expected, or later than expected, God's people will be found ready when Jesus comes.

Hymn of Response

On a hill far away stood an old rugged cross,
The emblem of suff'ring and shame;
And I love that old cross where the dearest and best
For a world of lost sinners was slain.

So I'll cherish the old rugged cross,
Till my trophies at last I lay down;
I will cling to the old rugged cross,
And exchange it some day for a crown.

Oh, that old rugged cross, so despised by the world,
Has a wondrous attraction for me;
For the dear Lamb of God left His glory above
To bear it to dark Calvary.

So I'll cherish the old rugged cross,
Till my trophies at last I lay down;
I will cling to the old rugged cross,
And exchange it some day for a crown.

In that old rugged cross, stained with blood so divine,
Such a wonderful beauty I see;
For 'twas on that old cross Jesus suffered and died,
To pardon and sanctify me.

So I'll cherish the old rugged cross,
Till my trophies at last I lay down;
I will cling to the old rugged cross,
And exchange it some day for a crown.

To that old rugged cross I will ever be true;
Its shame and reproach gladly bear.
Then He'll call me some day to my home far away,
Where his glory forever I'll share.

So I'll cherish the old rugged cross,
Till my trophies at last I lay down;
I will cling to the old rugged cross,
And exchange it some day for a crown.[32]

---

[32] George Bennard, "The Old Rugged Cross," 1913, *Baptist Hymnal*, #230.

CHAPTER 4

THE BETRAYAL OF JESUS CHRIST

"SILENT" WEDNESDAY: APRIL 5, AD 30

This is a short chapter because only one important event happened on Wednesday. After Tuesday's controversies and teaching, Jesus and his disciples appear to have spent Wednesday in Bethany. The Gospels do not record any activity by Jesus on that day, which is the reason the day is called "Silent Wednesday." Judas likely used this opportunity to venture the two miles into Jerusalem to meet with the chief priests and leaders to negotiate handing Jesus over to them. The chief priests must have been thrilled at his offer; the religious leaders had looked for this opening for a long time. Jesus's popularity with the crowds made it virtually impossible to seize him up to this point. Judas offered them the possibility to arrest him without the presence of the crowds (Mark 3:6; Luke 22:1–6).

Judas's motive is not perfectly clear. Jesus's approach to messiahship may have run contrary to Judas's dreams. Most first-century Jewish people thought the Messiah would be a militaristic warrior and establish an earthly kingdom, throwing off the yoke of Roman domination. Judas watched Jesus heal the sick, cast out demons, and raise the dead. When Jesus spoke on leadership, he painted a picture of service rather than domination. On one occasion, after the feeding of the five thousand, the crowd wanted to make him a king (John 6:15). Instead of accepting their offer, Jesus sent his disciples away while he went up on a mountain to pray (Matt 14:23). Judas may have expected that fame and fortune were on the horizon for the Messiah's disciples, but the more time passed the less likely that appeared to be true.

Judas's greed and thievery played an obvious role in his betrayal. On the previous Sabbath, Jesus rebuked Judas sternly for his criticism of Mary of Bethany (John 12:4–8). In that passage John made clear that Judas was a thief and pilfered out of the treasury. Certainly, Satan was at work in Judas. Judas's sins of thievery and greed made him an easy target for the devil.

The Synoptic Evangelists each record the meeting between Judas and the chief priests.[1] All three reference Judas as one of the Twelve. Judas's role as one of Jesus's closest followers heightens the duplicity of the betrayal. Judas's action was known well by the readers, but its inclusion drives home the point that the betrayal was an "inside job." Luke alone reveals that Satan entered Judas before he met with the chief priests (Luke 22:3). Behind the scenes a spiritual war was being fought; little did Satan know he was playing right into God's hand.

The chief priests and leaders must have been overjoyed to hear Judas say, "'What are you willing to give me if I hand him over to you?' So they weighed out thirty pieces of silver for him" (Matt 24:15). Mark and Luke indicate the chief priests gave Judas

---

[1] Matt 26:14–16; Mark 14:10–11; Luke 22:3–6.

money. Matthew alone specifies the amount as "thirty pieces of silver." In Exod 21:32 this is the price to be paid to the owner of a slave gored by another's ox. Joseph was sold by his brothers to the Midianites for twenty shekels (Gen 37:28). A shekel was worth four denarii, so thirty shekels would be worth approximately four months wages for a day laborer. The thirty pieces of silver is an allusion to Zech 11:12–13, which reads:

> Then I said to them, "If it seems right to you, give me my wages; but if not, keep them." So they weighed my wages, thirty pieces of silver.
>
> "Throw it to the potter," the LORD said to me—this magnificent price I was valued by them. So I took the thirty pieces of silver and threw it into the house of the LORD, to the potter.

This subtle but important allusion to Zechariah connects Judas's betrayal to Old Testament prophecy and continues the theme of God's sovereignty over the course of events, even the betrayal of Jesus. The thirty pieces of silver paid to Judas for betraying Jesus were returned to the temple and used to buy a potter's field (Matt 27:3–10).

Final Reflections

Whatever motivated Judas to betray Jesus, the act reminds us of how far one can go in religion and not be saved. Judas saw and heard things the Old Testament prophets longed to see and hear; yet, for whatever reason, he hardened his heart to the grace of God. The Bible makes clear Judas was responsible for his actions despite satanic involvement. At the end of the day, Judas failed to follow Jesus with wholehearted devotion. Today those who refuse to follow Jesus wholeheartedly and who embrace a "casual Christianity," which is not Christianity at all, are in danger of falling short of the grace of God. Some persons who attend church are much more enamored with their next vacation than serving the Lord in their local church. Others have chosen to allow their children's sporting events to continually trump their children's souls. While it is easy to condemn Judas for what he did, some Christians may need to reconsider how their lifestyle choices betray their commitment to Jesus Christ.

Hymn of Response

O sacred Head, now wounded,
with grief and shame weighed down,
now scornfully surrounded
with thorns, thine only crown!
O sacred Head, what glory,
what bliss till now was thine!
Yet, though despised and gory,
I joy to call thee mine.

What thou, my Lord, hast suffered
was all for sinners' gain.
Mine, mine was the transgression,
but thine the deadly pain.
Lo, here I fall, my Savior!
'Tis I deserve thy place.
Look on me with thy favor,
and grant to me thy grace.

What language shall I borrow
to thank thee, dearest Friend,

for this, thy dying sorrow,
thy pity without end?
Oh, make me thine forever,
and should I fainting be,
Lord, let me never, never
outlive my love to thee.

Be near when I am dying,
oh, show thy cross to me,
and for my rescue, flying,
come, Lord, and set me free!
These eyes, new faith receiving,
from Jesus shall not move,
for one who dies believing
dies safely, through thy love.[2]

---

[2] Paul Gerhardt, "O Sacred Head Now Wounded," trans. James W. Alexander, 1829, *Voices Together*, #325, Hymnary.org, https://hymnary.org /hymn/VT2020/325. This hymn is based on a medieval Latin poem often attributed to Bernard of Clairvaux or Arnulf of Leuven.

CHAPTER 5

THE LAST SUPPER

MAUNDY THURSDAY: APRIL 6, AD 30

Thursday of Passion Week is known as Maundy Thursday in many Christian traditions. The reason is that the Latin term for "new commandment" is *mandatum novum*. Jesus commanded his followers "to love one another" (John 13:34) on Thursday evening. The focus of the day is on Jesus's Last Supper with his disciples.[1] When exactly the events of Thursday night transitioned into the early morning hours of Friday is impossible to know for certain. At some point in the middle of Thursday night, Jesus was arrested in the garden of Gethsemane; taken to the home of Annas, the former high priest; and then brought to Caiaphas, the present high priest.

---

[1] Matt 26:17–35; Mark 14:12–32; Luke 22:7, 38; John 13:1–17:26.

Preparation for the Passover Meal[2]

When Jesus woke up Thursday morning, he would likely not close his eyes in sleep again until he closed them in death on Friday afternoon. He instructed Peter and John to make the necessary arrangements for celebrating the Passover meal (Luke 22:8).[3] The Synoptic Gospels present Jesus's final meal with his disciples as a Passover meal.[4] The beginning of the feast is referred to as the Feast of Unleavened Bread because the two feasts were celebrated concurrently in popular thinking.

Jesus's instructions demonstrate his omniscience in that he told the two disciples that when they entered the city, they would encounter a man carrying a jar of water. They were to follow the man to the house where they would eat the Passover meal. Finding a man carrying a jar of water would have been highly unusual, since it was considered "women's work."[5] The city would have been filled with tens of thousands of people preparing for Passover. The fact that Peter and John encountered the man who led them to the house where they were to

---

[2] Matt 26:17–19; Mark 14:12–16; Luke 22:7–13.

[3] On the Last Supper, see Nicholas Perrin, "Last Supper," in Green, *Dictionary of Jesus and the Gospels*, 2nd ed., 492–502.

[4] The issue of whether the Last Supper was a Passover meal is complex and the literature extensive. On the question, see Craig L. Blomberg, *The Historical Reliability of the New Testament* (Nashville: B&H Academic, 2016), 216–17. For an excellent evaluation of the various proposals, see Andreas J. Köstenberger, "Was the Last Supper a Passover Meal?" in *The Lord's Supper: Remembering and Proclaiming Christ until He Comes*, ed. Thomas R. Schreiner and Matthew R. Crawford (Nashville: B&H Academic, 2010), 6–30.

[5] Gen 24:11; John 4:7.

eat the Passover meal exhibits God's providence and Christ's omniscience.

Jesus certainly secured the room with the owner in advance. The enormous crowds would have made it difficult to obtain a place on short notice to celebrate the feast within the city walls. Peter and John found things just as Jesus told them. The entire discussion is reminiscent of the securing of the donkey for Jesus's triumphal entry.

Beginning of the Passover Meal[6]

Jesus and his disciples would have spent several hours together in the upper room. The events included: washing the disciples' feet, eating the Passover meal, a prediction of Peter's denials and Judas's betrayal, and a lengthy teaching session recorded by John.

Sometime around 6 p.m., Jesus and his disciples reclined around a U-shaped table.[7] What Jesus did next stunned his disciples.[8] Jesus knew the time for his departure had arrived. John does not say that Jesus was about to die but that he was about to return to the Father (John 13:1). He directs the reader's attention past the cross and to Jesus's triumphant return to the Father. There is not the slightest hint at the possibility of defeat. Jesus's love and commitment to his disciples was unquestioned: "He loved them to the end."

During the meal, the devil already had been at work in Judas (vv. 2, 27). John informed his readers earlier that Judas

---

[6] Matt 26:20; Mark 14:17; Luke 22:14–16; John 13:1–20, 27.

[7] Michael J. Wilkins, *Matthew*, Zondervan Illustrated Bible Backgrounds Commentary (Grand Rapids, MI: Zondervan, 2002), 164.

[8] John 13:1–17.

was a traitor and a thief (12:4, 6). At this sacred gathering a spiritual war was being waged. Despite Jesus's knowledge that he had all authority, and that he would soon return to his Father, he removed his outer garment, wrapped a towel around himself, poured water into a basin, and washed the disciples' feet—including those of Judas and Peter. The foot washing has theological importance as well as being a beautiful example of servant leadership.

A good host would provide a servant to wash his guests' feet; but if no servant were available, he would not do it himself. The exchange between Peter and Jesus reveals that the foot washing had symbolic significance beyond an act of humble service (13:6–9). Peter's resistance was met by an even stronger statement from Jesus: "If I don't wash you, you have no part with me" (v. 8). The reason for Jesus's strong response is that the foot washing was a window into the nature of the cleansing work of the cross.

Peter enthusiastically requested that Jesus wash his feet, hands, and head. Jesus changed his imagery slightly in his response to Peter. He made the point that God cleanses or bathes a person at conversion; but as the person lives in this fallen world, he or she picks up the world's dirt. What is needed is not another bath (conversion) but a cleansing of one's feet, confession of sin for a clean conscience and maintaining close fellowship with the Lord (1 John 1:9). The ominous tone of the evening continued as Jesus commented that not all of them were clean.

Jesus made a practical application from the foot washing. If he, as their Lord and Teacher, washed their feet, they should wash one another's feet (John 13:14). He made it perfectly clear that genuine blessing comes from obedience to his teaching and not just learning about it.

Identification of the Traitor[9]

We must always keep in mind that the Gospels give us various perspectives and summaries of what took place that night. These perspectives are complementary, not contradictory. They provide us with a more complete understanding of what Jesus said and did. Sometimes the Gospel writers arranged their material thematically and at other times chronologically. For example, Matthew and Mark describe Jesus's identification of the traitor before the meal, and Luke does so after the meal. For the most part, however, the synoptic authors present these events in parallel fashion.

Jesus made three prophecies: Judas's betrayal, the disciples' desertion, and Peter's denials, which would be fulfilled in very short order. Jesus demonstrated his awareness and control of everything taking place. While he went to his destiny forsaken and alone, he remained in sovereign control over everything.

The atmosphere in the upper room would have become extremely tense when Jesus revealed that one of them was a traitor. Judas must have been stunned to learn that his secret plan had been uncovered. The shocking revelation brought a flurry of responses from the disciples: "Surely not I?" Jesus made three things perfectly clear: first, the traitor was the one who dipped his hand in the dish with Jesus; second, that man would have been better off if he had never been born; and, third, this betrayal was ordained by God.

Jesus's comment that his betrayer was the one who dipped his hand in the bowl with Jesus would not have been as clear as it seems on the surface, for all of the disciples would have dipped

---

[9] Matt 26:21–25; Mark 14:18–21; Luke 22:21–23; John 13:21–30.

their hands in the bowl at some point. John's Gospel, however, describes the private conversation between Jesus and the beloved disciple (the apostle John) as to the identity of the traitor.

> "Lord, who is it?"
> Jesus replied, "He's the one I give the piece of bread to after I have dipped it." When he had dipped the bread, he gave it to Judas, Simon Iscariot's son. (John 13:25–26)

The terrible nature of Judas's treachery is seen in the way Jesus chose to describe his betrayal: **"The one who eats my bread has raised his heel against me"** (v. 18). Jesus was alluding to Ps 41:9, which says:

> Even my friend in whom I trusted,
> one who ate my bread,
> has raised his heel against me.

In this lament psalm, David decries the fact that a close friend, someone in whom he trusted and who ate with him (a sign of friendship) turned against him. David's sorrow is typologically related to that of the Davidic Messiah. Judas's betrayal was part of God's plan, written of long ago. The fact that the betrayal was the fulfillment of God's plan, having been prophesied in Scripture, but also the willful choice of the traitor, has puzzled students of the Bible throughout the centuries. Neither Jesus nor the Gospel writers explains how God's sovereignty and Judas's human responsibility can coexist; but both are stated without embarrassment.[10]

---

[10] For help on this topic, see the excellent work by D. A. Carson, *How Long, O Lord? Reflections on Suffering and Evil,* 2nd ed. (Downers Grove, IL: InterVarsity, 2006).

Jesus's death being "according to the Scriptures" (Mark 14:49) may be a reference to a passage like Isa 52:13–53:12. The "woe" pronounced by Jesus in Mark 14:21 is used in prophetic judgment oracles.[11] The emphasis is on the certainty of Judas's punishment. Before Judas left the meal to initiate Jesus's arrest, Satan entered him. Satan did not leave this to one of his demonic minions but involved himself actively in Judas's betrayal.[12]

The Last Supper

The Passover meal consisted of several basic elements, each one having symbolic importance and contributing to the retelling of the story of the exodus. The Passover lamb reminded the Jews of the lamb's blood smeared on the doorposts to escape the visitation of the angel of death. The unleavened bread reminded them of the swiftness of their redemption in that they had no time to bake bread before their flight. A bowl of fruit puree reminded them of the clay their ancestors used to make bricks during their captivity. The bowl of salt water recalled the tears of their slavery and the water of the Red Sea. The bitter herbs recalled the bitterness of the Israelites' bondage. Four cups of wine were consumed during the Passover meal. Each cup commemorated one of the four promises God made to his people:

> Therefore tell the Israelites: I am the Lord, and I will bring you out from the forced labor of the Egyptians

---

[11] For examples, see Isa 10:5 and Jer 23:1.

[12] For a fuller discussion of the role of Satan in Jesus's passion, see William F. Cook III and Chuck Lawless, *Spiritual Warfare in the Storyline of Scripture: A Biblical, Theological, and Practical Approach* (Nashville: B&H Academic, 2019).

and rescue you from slavery to them. I will redeem you with an outstretched arm and great acts of judgment. I will take you as my people, and I will be your God. You will know that I am the Lord your God, who brought you out from the forced labor of the Egyptians. (Exod 6:6–7)

The first Passover represented God's greatest act of deliverance in the Hebrew Scriptures and the creation of Israel as a nation. Yahweh defeated Pharaoh by his mighty power. He delivered his people from slavery through the sacrificial blood of a lamb. The Israelites were to kill a lamb and rub its blood on their doorframe: "The blood on the houses where you are staying will be a distinguishing mark for you; when I see the blood, I will pass over you. No plague will be among you to destroy you when I strike the land of Egypt" (12:13). The point is made a second time: "When the LORD passes through to strike Egypt and sees the blood on the lintel and the two doorposts, he will pass over the door and not let the destroyer enter your houses to strike you" (v. 23). The importance of this event cannot be overestimated. The killing of the firstborn was the straw that broke Pharaoh's back, so to speak, that resulted in the release of the Israelites from slavery and the dawning of a new covenant with their God. At the same time, it foreshadowed the death of Jesus, our Passover Lamb (John 1:29, 36; 1 Cor 5:7).

Later, when Israel was oppressed and defeated by her enemies, the prophets predicted a day when Yahweh would return to Zion to accomplish a new and greater exodus.[13] In light of

---

[13] See Isa 11:11–16; 35:1–10; 40:1–5; Jer 23:5–8; Hos 2:14–15.

this historical context, certain parallels between the Passover and the Last Supper become obvious. In the Passover, God remembered his covenant with Abraham. At the Lord's Supper a new covenant was established between God and his people. In the Passover, Israel remembered their bondage and slavery in Egypt and how God delivered them. At the Lord's Supper, believers are reminded of their former slavery to sin and Satan, but through Christ's death we receive forgiveness and freedom from bondage to sin. In the Passover, the blood of a Passover lamb was smeared on the doorpost of each family as a sign of obedience to God. A lamb had to die to secure the freedom of those inside the house. At the Lord's Supper, the blood of Christ, our Passover Lamb, has been shed. Jesus's words recall and transform the rich symbolism of Passover, announcing the arrival of the new exodus and the inauguration of the new covenant.

The Passover meal was conducted by prescribed order. First came a blessing for the festival and the first cup of wine, followed by drinking the first cup of wine. Next, the food would be brought out. The youngest son then asked why this night was different from all other nights. The father would answer the question by retelling the exodus story and pointing to the items on the table and their symbolic significance. Praise to God for past and future redemption followed the explanation, taken from the first part of the Hallel psalms (113–14). After drinking of the second cup of wine, the bread would be blessed, broken, and distributed. The bread would be eaten with the bitter herbs and the bowl of fruit puree. The meal was eaten next. The Passover meal included roasted lamb that had been sacrificed in the temple. At the conclusion of the meal, the father would bless a third cup of wine, which would be followed by singing the second part of the Hallel psalms (115–18). The fourth cup of wine concluded the meal.[14]

A comparison of the institution of the Lord's Supper in the Synoptic Gospels is on page 69.

Luke's account is slightly longer and will be the focus of my comments.[15] Jesus began by telling his closest companions how much he had longed to eat this meal with them before he suffered. His comment about his suffering increased the tension in the room. Jesus's statement, "For I tell you, I will not eat it again until it is fulfilled in the kingdom of God," directs the disciples' attention forward to his second coming and the messianic banquet.

Luke is the only evangelist to mention two cups of wine. The first mention is likely a reference to the first of the four cups: "I will bring you out from the forced labor of the Egyptians and rescue you from slavery to them" (Exod 6:6). The unleavened bread represents Jesus's body: "This is my body, which is given for you. Do this in remembrance of me" (Luke 22:19). [16]

---

[14] Mark L. Strauss, *Luke*, Zondervan Illustrated Bible Backgrounds Commentary (Grand Rapids, MI: Zondervan, 2015), 167.

[15] Luke 22:14–20.

[16] Jesus's words have been the source of much debate. The controversy centers on the interpretation of his statements, "This is my body . . . This is my blood." The Roman Catholic understanding is known as transubstantiation. Those who hold this view understand that when the priest speaks the appointed words, the bread and the wine are transformed into Jesus's body and blood. They maintain this position although the bread and wine physically remain bread and wine. A second understanding is associated with Lutheranism. The position is known as consubstantiation. This view teaches that the bread and wine remain bread and wine, but the spiritual presence of Christ's body and blood are present in, around, and through the elements. The Protestant interpretation understands Jesus's words in a

Matt 26:26–29	Mark 14:22–25	Luke 22:17–20	1 Cor 11:23–26
		17 Then he took a cup, and after giving thanks, he said, "Take this and share it among yourselves.	
		18 For I tell you, from now on I will not drink of the fruit of the vine until the kingdom of God comes."	
26 As they were eating, Jesus took bread, blessed and broke it, gave it to the disciples, and said, "Take and eat it; this is my body."	**22** As they were eating, he took bread, blessed and broke it, gave it to them, and said, "Take it; this is my body."	**19** And he took bread, gave thanks, broke it, gave it to them, and said, "This is my body, which is given for you. Do this in remembrance of me."	**23** For I received from the Lord what I also passed on to you: On the night when he was betrayed, the Lord Jesus took bread,
27 Then he took a cup, and after giving thanks, he gave it to them and said, "Drink from it, all of you.	**23** Then he took a cup, and after giving thanks, he gave it to them, and they all drank from it.	**20** In the same way he also took the cup after supper and said, "This cup is the new covenant in my blood, which is poured out for you."	**24** and when he had given thanks, broke it, and said, "This is my body, which is for you. Do this in remembrance of me."
28 For this is my blood of the covenant, which is poured out for many for the forgiveness of sins.	**24** He said to them, "This is my blood of the covenant, which is poured out for many.		**25** In the same way also he took the cup, after supper, and said, "This cup is in the new covenant in my blood. Do this, as often as you drink it, in remembrance of me."
29 But I tell you, I will not drink from this fruit of the vine from now on until that day when I drink it new with you in my Father's kingdom."	**25** Truly I tell you, I will no longer drink of the fruit of the vine until that day when I drink it new, in the kingdom of God."		**26** For as often as you eat this bread and drink the cup, you proclaim the Lord's death until he comes.

The wine represents the blood of the new covenant: "This cup is the new covenant in my blood, which is poured out for you" (22:20). Jesus's words echo Exod 24:8: "Moses took the blood, splattered it on the people, and said, 'This is the blood of the covenant that the LORD has made with you concerning all these words.'" The new covenant is a clear reference to Jer 31:31–34:

> "Look, the days are coming"—this is the LORD's declaration—"when I will make a new covenant with the house of Israel and with the house of Judah. This one will not be like the covenant I made with their ancestors on the day I took them by the hand to lead them out of the land of Egypt—my covenant that they broke even though I am their master"—the LORD's declaration. "Instead, this is the covenant I will make with the house of Israel after those days"—the LORD's declaration. "I will put my teaching within them and write it on their hearts. I will be their God, and they will be my people. No longer will one teach his neighbor or his brother, saying, 'Know the LORD,' for they will all know me, from the least to the greatest of them"—this is the LORD's declaration. "For I will forgive their iniquity and never again remember their sin."

---

more symbolic fashion, emphasizing the thought of remembrance, instead of focusing on the verb *is*. This position understands that what is taking place is essentially a memorial in which believers remember the work of Christ on the cross and look forward to his return. Within the Protestant position, some from the Reformed tradition understand that when the Lord's Supper is properly observed it is a means of grace to the believer, much like reading the Bible, prayer, or congregational worship.

While the Sinai covenant was established through the blood of sacrificial animals, the new covenant will be established through the blood of Jesus, God's beloved Son. Therefore, the most probable conclusion is that Jesus understood his death as a sacrifice of atonement, thereby establishing a new covenant with his people and leading them in a new exodus from bondage to Satan, sin, and death.

Finally, we must appropriate the meaning of the Lord's Supper personally. The supper itself does not have salvific power, but the aspect of personally eating the bread and drinking the cup suggests the necessity of personal faith in the death and resurrection of Jesus Christ. The blessings we commemorate in the Lord's Supper are applied to us personally by the Holy Spirit at conversion.

Greatness, Abandonment, and Denials[17]

At some point, likely shortly after the meal, the disciples argued over which one of them was the greatest (Luke 22:24–30). While this dispute seems like a most inappropriate topic in which to engage under the circumstances, they did the same after Jesus's second and third passion predictions (Mark 8:33–37; 10:35–45).

Jesus used the opportunity to teach, once again, on servant leadership. This approach to leadership is a very hard lesson to learn because the desire for prominence resides in even the best of hearts. The disciples had left everything to follow Jesus but failed to grasp his teaching on the issues of leadership and service. They thought about leadership from a worldly mindset— like the Gentiles whose rulers lorded over those under them. The

---

[17] Luke 22:24–38.

disciples viewed leadership from the perspective of being served, while Jesus set forth a completely different model. How quickly they forgot the fact that Jesus had just washed their feet! Jesus's standard of greatness stands in sharp contrast to the world's standard. The world's desire is to receive honor and acclaim, but Jesus wants his disciples to focus on service to people.

Jesus moved from the disciples' misconceptions concerning greatness to their falling away (Mark 14:27–31). This abandonment fulfills Zech 13:7: "Strike the shepherd, and the sheep will be scattered." The entire Zechariah passage reads:

> Sword, awake against my shepherd,
> against the man who is my associate—
>   this is the declaration of the LORD of Armies.
> Strike the shepherd, and the sheep will be scattered;
> I will turn my hand against the little ones.
> In the whole land—
>   this is the LORD's declaration—
> two-thirds will be cut off and die,
> but a third will be left in it.
> I will put this third through the fire;
> I will refine them as silver is refined
> and test them as gold is tested.
> They will call on my name,
> and I will answer them.
> I will say, "They are my people,"
> and they will say, "The LORD is our God." (Zech 13:7–9)

The reference to Zech 13:7 suggests Jesus's death was part of God's plan and demonstrates his sovereign control over what was about to transpire, even regarding the disciples' desertion of Jesus. The striking here is to be connected to the piercing of the messianic figure in Zech 12:10. This imagery may also be connected to Isa 53:4–5:

> Yet he himself bore our sicknesses,
> and he carried our pains;
> but we in turn regarded him stricken,
> struck down by God, and afflicted.
> But he was pierced because of our rebellion,
> crushed because of our iniquities;
> punishment for our peace was on him,
> and we are healed by his wounds.

Jesus clearly understood himself to be the Messiah-shepherd who was to die for sinners. The verb translated "scattered" or "fall away" (*skandalizō*) is used in Mark 4:17 in the parable of the soils: "But they have no root; they are short-lived. When distress or persecution comes because of the word, they immediately fall away."

Peter insisted he would not fall away. Jesus told him that before the rooster crowed twice, he would deny him three times. Jesus's words found fulfillment in just a matter of hours. Luke alone includes a reference to Jesus telling Peter that he had prayed for him. What a comfort to know Jesus prays for us even when we fail him. Jesus's graciousness is on full display here!

While Satan is not mentioned often in the Passion Narrative, the few references are significant and suggest a larger involvement "behind the scenes." John had already noted that Satan entered Judas after he took the bread from Jesus (John 13:27). Luke records Jesus's warning that Satan had asked permission to sift (*siniazō*)[18] the disciples as wheat. The imagery is a violent one

---

[18] Luke 22:31 is the only occurrence of this term (*hapax legomenon*) in the biblical corpus.

where a farmer separates the wheat from the chaff. Obviously, this took place beginning with Jesus's violent arrest and lasted until his glorious resurrection.

For Peter, this violent shaking can be seen in his three denials of Jesus. For the other disciples, their sifting began when they fled into the night and abandoned Jesus in the garden. Overwhelmed by fear, they decided to save themselves rather than fight for Jesus. Satan took advantage of the circumstances and brought tremendous demonic pressure on the disciples. Peter kept insisting that he would die rather than fall away. Jesus knew Peter (and us!) better than he knew himself. Peter was not alone in his audacity, as the others made the same promise. Once again, Jesus demonstrated his awareness of coming events.

Jesus's Farewell Discourse[19]

Imagine the thoughts running through the disciples' minds after Jesus told them that one of them was a traitor, their "unofficial" spokesman would desert him, and all of them would abandon him. If we did not have John's Gospel, we would know little of what Jesus taught in the upper room apart from his words concerning the Lord's Supper.

In the opening section of the discourse (John 14:1–31), Jesus explained why leaving the disciples was better for them than if he remained with them. He gave five reasons: (1) he was going

---

[19] Properly speaking John 14:1–16:33 is the Farewell Discourse, but I will include Jesus's prayer in this section as well (17:1–26). This discourse follows a literary form that was common in the ancient world, not least within Judaism. For an excellent exposition of the Farewell Discourse, see D. A. Carson, *The Farewell Discourse and Final Prayer of Jesus: An Evangelical Exposition of John 14–17* (Grand Rapids, MI: Baker, 1980).

to prepare a place for them (vv. 1–4); (2) he showed them the only way to the Father (vv. 5–7); (3) his departure would provide greater intimacy of relationship (vv. 8–11); (4) he would help them perform greater works (vv. 12–14); (5) he would send them another divine Helper (vv. 15–31).

Jesus's teaching in John 14–16 concerning the Holy Spirit is some of the most important in the Bible. During his absence, Jesus promised to send the Spirit as a Paraclete (*paraklētos*), meaning an "advocate" or "counselor." The Spirit would mediate the presence of the Father and the Son to the disciples—teaching, guiding, and comforting them (14:16–20, 26–27; 15:26–27; 16:5–16).

A key thought expressed in chapter 14 and repeated throughout the discourse is the close connection between love for Jesus and obedience to him. Jesus made it perfectly clear that heartfelt love cannot be separated from obedience. The person who obeys out of heartfelt devotion to Jesus will experience the love of God and the presence of Christ in a deeper way (14:21, 23).

The next section of the discourse (15:1–17) focuses on the relationship between Jesus and his followers as one of mutual indwelling—Christ in the believer and the believer in Christ. This passage can be divided into two parts. The two parts are not unrelated, as the terms "abide," "fruit," and "love" appear in both. In the first part Jesus established the close personal relationship that exists between himself and each believer (vv. 1–11). This mutual indwelling is illustrated in the imagery of the vine and branches. The second part focuses on the theme of love (vv. 12–17). Those who abide in Christ demonstrate their abiding by being people of Christian love, especially for fellow believers.

The third major section of the discourse (15:18–16:4) explains the world's hatred for Jesus's followers. This passage explains why loving one another was so important for Jesus's disciples. The world would hate them, persecute them, put them out of their synagogues, and try to kill them. They must love one another because the world would not love them. Jesus had stated elsewhere that his followers would be persecuted.[20] Ultimately the world hates God's people because the world hates Jesus. Concerning this hatred, God provides the Holy Spirit to aid them in the face of persecution (15:26–27).

The final section of the discourse (16:5–33) returns to the theme of Jesus's departure. Jesus encouraged the disciples that despite his return to the Father he would send the Spirit to them to turn their grief into joy and ensure their ultimate victory despite tribulation. We should be grateful to God for the Fourth Gospel, for without it we would know little of what Jesus taught his disciples in the upper room.

The discourse is followed by Jesus's famous prayer (17:1–26). Unlike the Synoptic Gospels, John does not describe Jesus's agonizing prayer in Gethsemane. Instead, John focuses on Jesus's prayer before arriving at the garden. You can learn a lot about a person by how, what, and when he or she prays. Jesus was unmistakably a man of prayer. Even now, at the Father's right hand, he intercedes for his people (Heb 7:25).

Jesus's prayer in John 17 is important for several reasons. First, we should understand what a magnificent privilege we have to "listen" to our Lord's heart as he prayed on the precipice of his horrific death. Second, Jesus prayed immediately after he told his disciples that in this world they would have tribulation (16:33). Shortly, he and his disciples would experience intense tribulation in the garden of Gethsemane. Third, his prayer reveals what was uppermost on his mind: the Father's glory (17:1–5); his disciples'

---

[20] See Matt 10:17–25; 24:9–14; Mark 13:9–13.

consecration, spiritual protection, and mission (vv. 6–19); and the unity, mission, and destiny of future believers (vv. 20–26).

As we read this prayer, we are truly astonished that it is not a gloomy prayer of hopelessness but instead a prayer of triumphant faith. This prayer reminds us that we live in a spiritual war zone. We must be on the alert for satanic attacks and the constant enticement of worldliness. We must never forget that "prayer is war" (Eph 6:18–20)!

Final Reflections

One of the most important themes in this chapter is the sovereignty of God. At every step along the way, we see God's will fulfilled. First, we find Jesus's instructions to the two disciples concerning the preparation for the Passover meal, from encountering a man carrying a jar of water to the man leading them to the home where the meal would be eaten. Second, the text reveals Jesus's prediction of the betrayal by Judas, and Jesus's foreknowledge that all his disciples would fall away, and Peter would deny him three times. Furthermore, at no point along the way would Jesus be caught unaware or would God's purposes be thwarted.

The principal objective of the Lord's Supper is to remind God's people of Christ's sacrifice for them on the cross ("Do this in remembrance of me"). God in his sovereignty ordained Christ's death during Passover to make it perfectly clear that Jesus's death was a Passover/salvific deliverance, freeing his people from bondage to Satan, sin, and the fear of death. Jesus's death brought about a "new exodus" for his people. The gift of his body and blood secured a new covenant relationship between God and his people. When the Lord's Supper is observed, sufficient time should be given to contemplate the utter sinfulness of sin. The bread and wine teach that Christ's atoning death is sufficient to pay the penalty for sin. The words of the old hymn written by Robert Lowry are powerfully true: "What can wash away my sin? Nothing but the blood of Jesus."

When the church celebrates the Lord's Supper, it is to look not only back to the cross but forward to Christ's second coming. Paul stated it this way in his letter to the Corinthians: "For as often as you eat this bread and drink the cup, you proclaim the Lord's death until he comes" (1 Cor 11:26). This brings a celebratory note to the Lord's Supper. Contemplating Christ's return, believers celebrate the truth that Jesus is coming again; and on that day, they will eat with him at the messianic banquet.

Hymn of Response

Amazing grace! how sweet the sound
That saved a wretch like me!
I once was lost, but now am found,
Was blind, but now I see.

'Twas grace that taught my heart to fear,
And grace my fears relieved;
How precious did that grace appear
The hour I first believed!

Through many dangers, toils and snares
I have already come;
'Tis grace hath brought me safe thus far,
And grace will lead me home.

The Lord has promised good to me,
His word my hope secures;

He will my shield and portion be
As long as life endures.

Yes, when this flesh and heart shall fail,
and mortal life shall cease:
I shall possess, within the veil,
a life of joy and peace.

The earth shall soon dissolve like snow,
the sun forbear to shine;
but God, who called me here below,
will be forever mine.[21]

---

[21] John Newton, "Amazing Grace," 1779, *Baptist Hymnal*, #104.

CHAPTER 6

The Garden of Gethsemane

Thursday Night–Early Hours of Friday Morning: April 6–7, AD 30

Jesus and the disciples departed the upper room and proceeded to the Garden of Gethsemane to begin the events that would reverse what happened in another garden, Eden. While the Synoptic Gospels describe Jesus's agonizing prayer in Gethsemane, John's account plunges immediately from Jesus's prayer in John 17 into his violent nighttime arrest.

Agony and Prayer[1]

The scene shifts dramatically from the upper room to a garden just outside Jerusalem. After singing a hymn Jesus and his disciples left Jerusalem through the Eastern Gate. They crossed the Kidron Valley and arrived at the lower western slopes of

---

[1] Matt 26:36–46; Mark 14:32–42; Luke 22:40–46.

the Mount of Olives. They proceeded to Gethsemane, a garden or orchard, and one of Jesus's favorite places to visit when in Jerusalem (John 18:2).[2] The name means "oil press." The significance of the moment is indicated by Jesus taking his inner circle—Peter, James, and John—with him to pray.

The Synoptic Gospels describe Jesus's agony in prayer with shocking boldness. Jesus said to his inner circle, "'I am deeply grieved to the point of death. Remain here and stay awake.' He went a little farther, fell to the ground, and prayed that if it were possible, the hour might pass from him. And he said, '*Abba*, Father! All things are possible for you. Take this cup away from me'" (Mark 14:34–36). Luke adds, "Being in anguish, he prayed more fervently, and his sweat became like drops of blood falling to the ground" (Luke 22:44). Luke appears to be saying that Jesus's sweat was *like* drops of blood, rather than actually dripping drops of blood from his forehead. If that was the case, then his sweat drops were large and profuse.

One wonders what was happening there. Jesus's response is stunning and completely unexpected. From Caesarea Philippi through the Last Supper, Jesus stated his intention to die. Was he now having second thoughts? Was Jesus suddenly afraid to die? In my mind, this thought seems ridiculous. If Jesus feared dying, he would not have confronted the religious establishment as boldly and repeatedly as he did. Furthermore, he would not have returned to Jerusalem, for he knew the religious leaders wanted to kill him. Did Jesus fear events in the garden would get out of control and he would be killed there before the cross? I find this equally unlikely. Jesus predicted his death by crucifixion

---

[2] See Joel B. Green, "Gethsemane," in Green, *Dictionary of Jesus and the Gospels*, 2nd ed., 309–13 (see chap. 1, n. 2).

on numerous occasions and never wavered from this conviction. He responded as he did because he was facing the reality that in a few hours he would bear humanity's sins in his body and suffer his Father's wrath. Jesus's words from the cross express the horror he faced: "My God, my God, why have you abandoned me?" (Matt 27:46). Jesus never sinned—not in thought, word, or deed. Now he would bear in his body humanity's sins. The following three passages capture the essence of this thought:

> He himself bore our sins in his body on the tree; so that, having died to sins, we might live for righteousness. (1 Pet 2:24)

> He made the one who did not know sin to be sin for us, so that in him we might become the righteousness of God. (2 Cor 5:21)

> Christ redeemed us from the curse of the law by becoming a curse for us, because it is written, **Cursed is everyone who is hung on a tree.** (Gal 3:13)

Jesus encouraged his disciples to remain with him and to stay awake. He collapsed on the ground as he began to pray. He addressed God as "*Abba*, Father" (Mark 14:36). "Abba" is an affectionate and reverential address of a Jewish child, or even an adult, to their father. Jesus prayed that, if possible, God would remove the cup from him, but he immediately added, "Nevertheless, not what I will, but what you will" (Mark 14:36). The cup of which Jesus spoke is the cup of God's wrath—his righteous indignation against sin. A few passages that give us insight into the cup are as follows:

> Therefore, this is what the LORD of Armies says concerning the prophets:

> I am about to feed them wormwood
> and give them poisoned water to drink,
> for from the prophets of Jerusalem
> ungodliness has spread throughout the land. (Jer 23:15)

This is what the LORD, the God of Israel, said to me: "Take this cup of the wine of wrath from my hand and make all the nations to whom I am sending you drink from it." (Jer 25:15)

> Wake yourself, wake yourself up!
> Stand up, Jerusalem,
> you who have drunk the cup of his fury
> from the LORD's hand;
> you who have drunk the goblet to the dregs—
> the cup that causes people to stagger. (Isa 51:17)

Jesus affirmed God's omnipotence when he prayed, "All things are possible for you," demonstrating his absolute confidence in God's power. His request that the Father "take this cup away from me," in the context of the Gospels, is a bold and striking request. Jesus had demonstrated throughout his ministry his determination to drink the cup. His words, however, are a beautiful example of genuine honesty in prayer.

Jesus's submission to the Father's will was not words spoken by an ivory-tower theologian but the words of one who prayed with the profound conviction that God's will is always best. Jesus prayed for something God could not answer affirmatively— "take this cup away." God's answer came through the unfolding events—betrayal, arrest, abandonment, denial, beatings, trial, mockery, crucifixion, and death.

Jesus's agony must have been increased greatly by the sleeping of the disciples. Jesus's comment about temptation reveals that what took place was more than just dying; he was engaged in a battle with Satan himself. The disciples, however, were "flesh" dominated (Mark 14:38).

Jesus brought out the relationship between the present circumstances and demonic activity in his statement, "Pray that you may not fall into temptation" (Luke 22:40). While Matthew and Mark record Jesus saying this once, Luke records it twice, at the beginning and ending of the prayer in the garden (vv. 40, 46). Jesus's warning about falling into temptation because of prayerlessness played out in his arrest. The disciples would flee into the night, abandoning Jesus, while Jesus stood strong in the face of temptation (Mark 14:50). At no point while in the garden did Jesus ask his disciples to pray for him.

The Mark passage crescendos in verses 41 and 42 with three fateful forces coming together: (1) "The time has come"; (2) "The Son of Man is betrayed"; and (3) "My betrayer is near." Jesus instructed the disciples to rise from their slumber. Jesus's time of prayer steeled him to follow God's plan through to the end. Despite their secret plot, Jesus's opponents did not take him by surprise.

Jesus's Betrayal and Arrest[3]

The Synoptics and John's accounts focus on different aspects of the events surrounding Jesus's arrest. Once again, we see these as complementary rather than contradictory. John focuses on

---

[3] Matt 26:47–56; Mark 14:43–52; Luke 22:47–53; John 18:1–11.

Jesus's protection of his disciples, as he demonstrated himself to be the Good Shepherd. The Synoptics, however, focus on Judas's betrayal with a kiss, the commotion surrounding the arrest, and the disciples' flight into the darkness. All four Gospels depict the mob sent to arrest Jesus as well as the incident involving Peter and Malchus's severed ear.

Jesus's previous statement from Mark 14:42, "Get up; let's go. See, my betrayer is near," is confirmed in verse 43. Mark ties together Jesus's Gethsemane prayer and his arrest—"While he was still speaking." The drama of the arrest escalates with the description of the forces arrayed against Jesus: a fallen disciple, the violent power of Rome, and the hatred of the religious authorities.[4] Judas was out in front of the mob. Judas reminds us of the danger of failing to take advantage of one's spiritual privileges. He spent approximately three years as Jesus's disciple. He heard Jesus teach. He saw Jesus perform miracles. But now he was leading Jesus's enemies into the garden to arrest Jesus. The lanterns and torches (John 18:3) were necessary, even with the full moon of Passover, in case Jesus and his followers fled into the darkness.

The sign of betrayal was to be a kiss. Both Matthew and Mark tersely describe this event.[5] A sign of identification may have been necessary since not everyone present had seen Jesus's face. Judas greeted Jesus by calling him "Rabbi" and kissing

---

[4] Only John mentions the presence of Roman soldiers (John 18:3). The term "company" (*spira*), in theory, was a thousand soldiers. The term could also refer to two hundred soldiers. While this seems to be a large number for such a task, we must remember that the Romans were very cautious to prevent an uprising during the Passover. Note that 470 soldiers guarded Paul on his journey from Jerusalem to Caesarea (Acts 23:23).

[5] John's Gospel does not mention Judas's kiss.

him—a chilling depiction of the betrayal of a friend.[6] A sign of love was transformed into something sinister. The treacherous use of a kiss is found in other places in the Bible, as in the story of Absalom ingratiating himself to those coming to see David and in Joab's killing of Amasa (2 Sam 15:5; 20:8–10). The author of Proverbs notes, "The kisses of an enemy are excessive" (27:6).

At the very moment when one might expect an unarmed victim to flee, John portrays Jesus in complete control. His enemies fell to the ground as he identified himself as the divine "I am" (John 18:6). Knowing exactly what happened is difficult; but that they were startled and one tumbled over another in a domino effect seems unlikely. John, however, makes clear that they "stepped back and fell to the ground" in response to Jesus's "I am he" (*egō eimi*) statement.[7] Something dramatic and dynamic happened when Jesus spoke these words. We should understand this event along the lines of a theophany—a manifestation of God. We must not necessarily conclude, however, that the soldiers understood what took place.

Jesus identified himself again to his enemies and demanded that his disciples be permitted to leave (v. 8). John, in contrast to the Synoptics, does not describe the disciples fleeing into the darkness. Instead, John focuses on Jesus, as the Good Shepherd, offering himself in their place. We should never underestimate the tender concern Jesus has for his followers. Jesus's actions fulfill his earlier promise to lose none of those given to him by the

---

[6] On Judas, see David J. Williams, "Judas Iscariot," in Green, McKnight, and Marshall, *Dictionary of Jesus and the Gospels*, 406–8 (see chap. 1, n. 16).

[7] Falling to the ground in God's presence is a common reaction in the Bible. See Ezek 1:28; 44:4; Dan 2:46; 8:18; 10:9; Acts 9:4; 22:7; Rev 1:17; 19:10; 22:8.

Father (17:12). If ever there was a moment when Jesus could be excused for acting selfishly, this was that moment. But he thought only of his disciples. The passage reminds us of the voluntary nature of Jesus's suffering. If in this vulnerable moment his enemies were overwhelmed by his presence, there can be no doubt that he willingly submitted himself to be taken captive by them and suffer crucifixion at their hands.

The brevity of the words veils what took place next. The Synoptic writers do not mention the name of the culprit who wielded the sword (*machaira*) or the identity of the one whose ear was partially cut off. John, writing approximately twenty-five to thirty years later, indicates that the servant's name was Malchus and that Peter performed the act of violence. Luke, the beloved physician, is the only Gospel writer to describe Jesus healing Malchus's ear (Luke 22:51). Jesus not only taught his followers to love their enemies (6:27), he practiced it himself.

Jesus's words draw attention to the stark difference between his integrity and the lack of integrity in his opponents—"Have you come out with swords and clubs, as if I were a criminal, to capture me? Every day I was among you, teaching in the temple, and you did not arrest me. But the Scriptures must be fulfilled" (Mark 14:48–49). They came out on Passover evening to arrest Jesus as if he were a common thief. In contrast, he taught openly in the temple courts. His words contrast his bravery with their cowardice.

Jesus understood this horrible moment as fulfilling the Scriptures. He may be alluding here to Zech 13:7, which he referenced earlier: "Strike the shepherd, and the sheep will be scattered; / I will turn my hand against the little ones." It is also possible we should understand "Scriptures" not as a reference to some specific texts in which the moment of arrest is prophesied, but to the entire salvific intent of God, which the early church saw woven throughout the Old Testament.

When all hope appeared lost, the disciples abandoned Jesus, fleeing into the darkness. Yet, before we are too critical of the disciples, we must realize that we would have done the exact same thing. Mark concludes this scene of mob violence with a bizarre epilogue describing an unnamed young man fleeing into the night (Mark 14:51–52). This event has been interpreted in various ways. Some consider the incident to be symbolic. Mark uses the identical term "young man" (*neaniskos*) in Mark 16:5 to describe the figure who greeted the women at the empty tomb. The "linen cloth" (*sindōn*) is the word used to describe Jesus's burial cloth in Mark 15:46. Therefore, some suggest that this strange incident in the garden is a symbolic prelude to the resurrection story. As Jesus is arrested, the narrative flashes ahead to the empty tomb story. Jesus will ultimately escape the clutches of death in resurrection, shedding his burial garments as the young man does in the garden. However, this understanding seems highly unlikely since the narrative appears to be a straightforward report of an actual historical event.

Certainly, this incident communicates the terrible confusion taking place as Jesus was arrested. Although Mark does not identify the young man, the anonymity may suggest that the young man is John Mark himself. But there is no way to know this for certain. The fine linen garment may indicate that the youth was from a wealthy family. He escaped naked, which indicates that he dressed hastily to follow Jesus and the disciples to the garden.

Final Reflections

The events in the garden leave the reader breathless. Jesus's deep anguish of soul is unexpected, his prayer that the cup be taken from him unforeseen, the betrayal of a friend unthinkable, the abandonment of his disciples shocking, and his nighttime arrest like a common criminal unimaginable. How could this series of events be God's plan, God's will? Yet, God's ways are not our ways, and his thoughts are much higher than our thoughts (Isa 55:8–9). As Jesus stood before his captors, he was not alone; his Abba, Father was with him.

A casual observer could only conclude that the best of plans had gone awry. He or she would fail to see that when Jesus prayed "your will be done," everything taking place was part of God's will. This observer would also fail to see that behind the scenes a spiritual war was taking place. When Jesus exhorted his disciples to pray that they would not fall into temptation, he was serious. Earlier that evening, Satan entered Judas (John 13:27). While Jesus was being arrested, he told his captors, "This is your hour—and the dominion of darkness" (Luke 22:53). All that human eyes could see was a solitary man being abandoned by his friends. We should be reminded that things are not always as they appear. When we think God has lost control of the circumstances of our lives, we must remember he sits on heaven's throne!

Reading about Jesus's season of intense darkness helps us understand why he can comfort us in our own hours of great darkness. As his disciples we must learn we are never safer than when we embrace God's will, even when we cannot see where he is taking us. In the dark of the night, we should pour out our hearts to God, as Jesus did. But before we say amen, we should pray as Jesus did with all sincerity, Not my will but your will be done.

The most important lesson to learn from Gethsemane is not about us but about Jesus. The most important lesson is Christological. As we have seen, Jesus was not afraid to die; he dreaded the thought of separation from his Father. When Jesus prayed, "Let this cup pass from me" (Matt 26:39), his words foreshadowed his cry from the cross, "My God, my God, why have you abandoned me?" (Mark 15:34). While he never sinned, on the cross he became sin for us (2 Cor 5:21). What love Jesus has for his people! Out of the darkest of nights, God's love won out!

Hymn of Response

Alas, and did my Savior bleed,
And did my Sov'reign die?
Would He devote that sacred head
For sinners such as I?

Chorus:
At the cross, at the cross where I first saw the light,
And the burden of my heart rolled away,
It was there by faith I received my sight,
And now I am happy all the day!

Was it for crimes that I had done
He groaned upon the tree?
Amazing pity, grace unknown,
And love beyond degree!

Chorus:
At the cross, at the cross where I first saw the light,
And the burden of my heart rolled away,
It was there by faith I received my sight,
And now I am happy all the day!

Well might the sun in darkness hide,
And shut His glories in

When Christ, the mighty Maker, died
For man, the creature's sin.

Chorus:
At the cross, at the cross where I first saw the light,
And the burden of my heart rolled away,
It was there by faith I received my sight,
And now I am happy all the day!

Thus might I hide my blushing face
While Cal'vry's cross appears,
Dissolve my heart in thankfulness,
And melt mine eyes to tears.

Chorus:
At the cross, at the cross where I first saw the light,
And the burden of my heart rolled away,
It was there by faith I received my sight,
And now I am happy all the day!

But drops of tears can ne'er repay
The debt of love I owe;
Here, Lord, I give myself away,
'Tis all that I can do.

Chorus:
At the cross, at the cross where I first saw the light,
And the burden of my heart rolled away,
It was there by faith I received my sight,
And now I am happy all the day![8]

---

[8] Isaac Watts and Ralph E. Hudson, "At the Cross," 1707, *Baptist Hymnal*, #255.

CHAPTER 7

THE JEWISH TRIAL: GUILTY OF BLASPHEMY

EARLY HOURS OF FRIDAY: APRIL 7, AD 30

The next several hours must have seemed like a whirlwind to Jesus. After his nighttime arrest, he was taken before the Jewish leadership. They had waited for this opportunity since early in Jesus's ministry. Now, in the middle of the night, only hours after celebrating the Passover, their opportunity had arrived. While Jerusalem and its Passover pilgrims slept, Jesus was standing trial for his life. His Jewish captors would condemn him for blasphemy and then send him to the Roman governor. They could not have imagined how difficult it would be to get Pilate to condemn Jesus to death.[1]

---

[1] On Jesus's trial, see Lynn H. Cohick, "Trial of Jesus," in Green, *Dictionary of Jesus and the Gospels*, 2nd ed., 972–79 (see chap. 1, n. 2).

Jesus's Jewish Trial[2]

The Gospel accounts of Jesus's trials prove difficult to harmonize in places. John, in contrast to the Synoptics, refers to Jesus being taken immediately to Annas after his arrest in the garden (John 18:13). Matthew and Mark seem to reference two trials, one in the middle of the night and another at daybreak. Luke describes only the one at daybreak. In light of the evidence, I understand there to have been three phases to Jesus's Jewish trial: before Annas (only described by John); before Caiaphas and at least a portion of the Sanhedrin in the middle of the night; and then at daybreak a third phase, with a final review of the testimony.

Difficulties also exist in the Gospels' presentations of Peter's denials. Luke chooses to present Peter's denials first and then give his summary of Jesus's examination. Matthew and Mark describe Peter's denials after their presentation of Jesus's examinations. John intersperses the denials with the interrogation before Annas (John 18:17, 25–27). While making a final determination on Peter's denials is not easy, I believe the various perspectives arise due to each of the evangelists' narrative purposes. Several of the choices appear to be the authors' attempts to contrast Jesus and Peter.

Some scholars argue that Jesus could not have stood trial before the Sanhedrin. Later Jewish texts strictly forbade many of the procedures described in the Gospels.[3] The following list highlights some of these concerns.

---

[2] Matt 26:57–68; Mark 14:53–55; Luke 22:54; John 18:12–27.

[3] For a comprehensive examination of the Jewish trial scene, including a fuller discussion of these issues related to historicity, see Raymond E. Brown, *The Death of the Messiah: From Gethsemane to the Grave* (New York: Doubleday, 1994), 1:315–560; Josef Blinzler, *The Trial of Jesus: The Jewish*

- The trial was held at night and in the home of the high priest (rather than in the official court of the Sanhedrin).
- The trial was held on the Passover, and trials were forbidden on the Sabbath and feast days.
- The testimony of the witnesses did not agree, whereas the law demanded scrupulous agreement among witnesses.
- The sentence of death followed immediately after the proceeding, whereas later law demanded that a period must intervene.
- Some suggest the event may have been nothing more than a preliminary interrogation as part of a strategy session before bringing Jesus to Pilate. This strategy would have involved a small number of Jewish leaders but not the entire Sanhedrin. The Jewish trial scene then developed later under the influence of the Roman trial scene.
- Jesus was condemned for blasphemy, but blasphemy referred to pronouncing the divine name.

Responses to These Concerns:

- Debate exists as to whether these later stipulations were practiced in the first third of the first century. As far as we know, a very different atmosphere likely prevailed prior to AD 70.
- The later legislation found in the Mishnah is based on Pharisaic tradition; but at this time, the Sadducees dominated the Sanhedrin.

---

and Roman Proceedings Against Jesus Christ (Ireland: Newman Press, 1959); and Schnabel, *Jesus in Jerusalem*, 249–67 (see chap. 1, n. 10).

- At the end of the day, this situation may be nothing more than a case of frantic people responding to desperate times. The longer the religious leaders waited, the greater the possibility that those who supported Jesus would come to his defense. What they intended to do, they needed to do quickly.

Matthew and Mark give the impression that Jesus was involved in a trial. They called witnesses, made charges, interrogated Jesus, convicted him of blasphemy, and condemned him to death. This process sounds very much like a trial.

Jesus's trial before his Jewish captors unfolded in three phases. Jesus was first taken to Annas, a former Jewish high priest and the father-in-law of Caiaphas, the present high priest. After a brief time before Annas, Jesus was taken before the Sanhedrin in the middle of the night. At daybreak, the council reconvened and condemned Jesus to death, after which they sent him to the Roman governor.

Phase One: Jesus before Annas[4]

The setting changed dramatically when Jesus was arrested in the garden and dragged before Annas. We can easily understand why Jesus was brought initially to Annas—he was one of the most powerful men in Jerusalem. He was a former high priest; five of his sons and his son-in-law (Caiaphas) followed him in that position. Jesus was likely taken to Annas both out of deference to his position and to allow Caiaphas time to gather the ruling council.

Annas focused his questioning of Jesus on two topics: Jesus's disciples and his teaching. Jesus took the focus off the disciples

---

[4] John 18:12–27.

and commented that his teaching was done in the open. He was struck by one of the attendants, who accused him of showing disrespect to Annas. Jesus demanded that proper judicial practice be followed, such as the calling of witnesses. The scene concludes with Annas sending Jesus to Caiaphas (John 18:24). John, however, does not describe the actual encounter between Jesus and the Sanhedrin but proceeds to describe Peter's denials and then moves on to Jesus's trial before Pilate.

Phase Two: Jesus before the Sanhedrin in the Middle of the Night[5]

Jesus was taken from the home of Annas to the residence of Caiaphas. The two homes may have been side by side and connected by a common courtyard. Jesus had now come face-to-face with his most hostile adversaries. The Sanhedrin appeared to be in a panic, seeking witnesses to testify against Jesus. As the proceeding continued, attempts were made to muster false witnesses against him. Jewish law stated that at least two, preferably three, witnesses had to agree before the death penalty could be imposed: "The one condemned to die is to be executed on the testimony of two or three witnesses. No one is to be executed on the testimony of a single witness" (Deut 17:6).[6]

One major accusation against Jesus was his alleged threats against the temple. The Jewish leaders misunderstood something Jesus had said a few years earlier: "Destroy this temple [his body], and I will raise it up [his resurrection] in three days" (John 2:19). No matter how hard the Jews tried, they continued to bungle

---

[5] Matt 26:57–68; Mark 14:53–65; Luke 22:54.
[6] See also Num 35:30 and Deut 19:15.

the entire proceedings. We should not be surprised by their lies. Earlier in Jesus's ministry, he referred to them as children of the devil, the father of lies: "You are of your father the devil, and you want to carry out your father's desires. He was a murderer from the beginning and does not stand in the truth, because there is no truth in him. When he tells a lie, he speaks from his own nature, because he is a liar and the father of lies" (John 8:44).

Jesus's refusal to respond to their false accusation frustrated his interrogators. His silence is reminiscent of Isaiah 53:7:

> He was oppressed and afflicted,
> yet he did not open his mouth.
> Like a lamb led to the slaughter
> and like a sheep silent before her shearers,
> he did not open his mouth.

Jesus's continued silence ushered the proceedings into the climax of the trial when the high priest stood and said to Jesus, "Don't you have an answer to what these men are testifying against you?" Jesus remained silent as the high priest continued, "I charge you under oath by the living God: Tell us if you are the Messiah, the Son of God" (Matt 26:62–63). Jesus's response in Mark's Gospel is an immediate and unqualified affirmative: "I am" (Mark 14:62).[7] In Matthew 26:64 Jesus brought together imagery from Dan 7:13 and Ps 110:1, saying, "you will see **the Son of Man seated at the right hand** of Power **and coming on the clouds of heaven.**"

Jesus's words are a dramatic declaration of coming victory. The irony is that the council thought they were judging Jesus, but Jesus

---

[7] While Jesus's response in Matthew seems less direct, obviously Caiaphas took it as an affirmation.

was actually their eschatological judge. What happened next was nothing less than an expression of undiluted hatred. The high priest tearing his garment was a sign of contempt, expressing the fact that he regarded Jesus's answer to be blasphemous (Matt 26:65).[8]

The question must be asked, What did Jesus say that caused them to accuse him of blasphemy? According to later rabbinic writings (m. Sanhedrin 7:5), someone was not technically guilty of blasphemy unless that person pronounced the divine name.[9] Various suggestions have been offered:

- Jesus's claim to be the Messiah
- Jesus's claim to be the Son of God
- The comment Jesus supposedly made against the temple
- Jesus's use of the divine name when he replied, "I am"
- Jesus's claim to sit at God's right hand

Of these, the final suggestion appears to be the most likely. We should not assume that the narrow definition of blasphemy found in the Mishnah was in effect in Jesus's day. While we should not think that the Sanhedrin thought Jesus was making a trinitarian kind of statement, we can reasonably assume he was putting himself in a relationship with God that was different from every other person's. Jesus had been accused of committing blasphemy earlier in his ministry when he declared that a healed paralytic's sins were forgiven (Mark 2:9). The mockery and physical abuse against Jesus jolt us back to the reality of the moment—the sinless Son of God is on trial for his life before those committed to killing him.

---

[8] Joshua and Caleb tore their clothes in response to the cowardice of the other ten spies (Num 14:6).

[9] For a more complete discussion on the charge of blasphemy see Brown, *Death of the Messiah*, 1:520–27.

Phase Three: Jesus before the Sanhedrin at Daybreak[10]

The Council reconvened at the break of day to solidify their findings before sending Jesus to Pontius Pilate. Luke focuses his trial scene on this early morning meeting. Once again, Jesus was questioned concerning his messiahship. His response demonstrates his courage in the face of intense hatred. The exchange was brief but heated: "But he said to them, 'If I do tell you, you will not believe. And if I ask you, you will not answer. But from now on, the Son of Man will be seated at the right hand of the power of God.' They all asked, 'Are you, then, the Son of God?' And he said to them, 'You say that I am'" (Luke 22:67–70).

While Jesus's response appears less than a strong affirmation, the Sanhedrin did not take it that way. We should understand Jesus's reply to have more to do with their inability to grasp the full import of his claims. The response by the Sanhedrin was immediate and decisive. They condemned Jesus to death. The Sanhedrin heard all they needed to hear. They had waited for this opportunity a long time, and here they had the evidence from his own mouth. Now they faced the difficult task of convincing the Roman governor Pontius Pilate that Jesus deserved to die.

Peter's Denials[11]

Peter's denials must have made a big impression on the early church, evidenced by the fact that they are described in all four Gospels. After Jesus, no person is mentioned in the Gospels more than Peter. John's Gospel describes Peter's introduction to Jesus

---

[10] Matt 27:1; Mark 15:1a; Luke 22:66–71.
[11] Matt 26:69–75; Mark 14:66–72; Luke 22:55–65; John 18:25–27.

by his brother Andrew (John 1:40–42). Peter was the spokes-person for the Twelve at Caesarea Philippi, where he confessed Jesus to be the Christ (Mark 8:29). He was on the Mount of Transfiguration with Jesus, James, and John (9:2–9). In the upper room, Peter declared boldly that he would die for Jesus rather than deny him (14:31). Luke alone records the reference to Satan demanding permission to sift Peter (and the other disciples) like wheat (Luke 22:31–34). This scene depicts that sifting.

After Jesus's arrest, Peter followed from a distance. Another disciple—likely John—helped him gain access to the high priest's courtyard. A servant girl of the high priest recognized Peter as one of Jesus's disciples. Peter denied understanding or even knowing what she was talking about, and then a rooster crowed. Next, the girl spoke her accusation to others. Again, Peter denied knowing Jesus. Galileans were easily identified by their dialect, and Peter's speech revealed his Galilean origins. The force of Peter's third denial is shocking: "Then he started to curse and swear, 'I don't know this man you're talking about!'" (Mark 14:71). Just as he finished speaking, a rooster crowed, and Peter suddenly remembered Jesus's prophecy that he would deny him. Luke indicates that Jesus turned and locked eyes with Peter at this exact moment (Luke 22:61). Overwhelmed by shame and guilt, Peter ran into the darkness weeping.

The Death of Judas[12]

Matthew alone describes Judas's remorse and suicide (Matt 27:3–5). He places it between Jesus's Jewish and Roman trials, although knowing the chronology of this event with certainty is

---

[12] Matt 27:3–10; Acts 1:16–19.

difficult. Its present placement could be intended by Matthew to draw a stark contrast between Peter's weeping and Judas's suicide.

Why was Judas surprised and filled with remorse at the reality that Jesus was condemned to death by the Sanhedrin? What did he expect they would do? They had wanted to kill Jesus for a long time. Judas's remorse may be nothing more than he came to his senses, having betrayed one who did so much for him. Much has been made of the word Matthew chose to express Judas's "remorse" (*metamelomai*), instead of the more common word to characterize repentance (*metanoia*). While the distinction in words is not insignificant, it is more helpful to understand that Judas's remorse did not lead him to seek forgiveness from Jesus (which in the moment would have been impossible) or reconciliation with the other disciples. Rather, Judas took his own life; he was swallowed up in hopelessness. The betrayal of "innocent blood" (v. 4) was more than he could bear.

The chief priests and elders had no more sympathy for Judas than they had for Jesus. Their only interest in Judas had been to get information from him so they could seize Jesus apart from the crowds. They had no further use for him. Judas responded to their callousness by throwing (*rhiptō*, a strong term) the thirty pieces of silver into the temple. Matthew then recounts Judas's death in the briefest of terms: "Then he went and hanged himself" (v. 5).

The utter hypocrisy of the chief priests and elders was on full display when they determined they could not keep the "blood money" (v. 6), which they paid, although they had just condemned an innocent man. After conferring, they took the money and bought a field for the burial of foreigners—likely Jews from the Diaspora who died during a visit to Jerusalem. The plot of land was still referred to as the "Field of Blood" when Matthew wrote his Gospel (v. 8).

Matthew understood these events (the death of Judas and the purchase of the field) as fulfilling the prophecy of Jeremiah. The major portion of the text, however, comes from Zech 11:12–13, with an additional allusion to Jer 19:1–13. Combining two or more Old Testament citations into one text is not unusual. Usually, when this situation occurs, only the more prominent prophet is mentioned.[13]

Matthew interprets these passages typologically. He did not make up the story based on the Zechariah text, but he read the prophet with a view of finding patterns in which an Old Testament person or event anticipated something in Jesus's life and ministry. D. A. Carson notes that Matthew saw in Jeremiah 19 and Zechariah 11 "a pattern of apostasy and rejection that must find its ultimate fulfillment in the rejection of Jesus."[14] With this concept of prophetic fulfillment comes the implicit corollary of God's sovereignty guiding these prophetic events.

One final issue to consider with the death of Judas is the seemingly contradictory presentations in Matthew and Acts. While Matthew describes Judas's remorse and hanging of himself, Acts describes Judas falling headlong and his body bursting open (1:18). However, the two accounts are complementary retellings of the same event, each focusing on different aspects of Judas's death. Both accounts include Judas's purchase of a field with his "unrighteous wages" and the land known as "the Field of Blood" (Matt 27:3–10; Acts 1:16–19). Imagine how the rope Judas used to hang himself or a branch to which the rope

---

[13] For example, Mark 1:2 quotes Malachi and Isaiah but refers only to Isaiah, the more prominent prophet.

[14] Carson, *Matthew*, 566 (see chap. 3, n. 19).

was tied may have broken, with his body hanging over the edge of a cliff and falling onto sharp rocks below. If Judas had been dead for some time, his body would have been in the process of decomposition, and the bodily fluids would likely have been released in the fall. If this scenario is correct, then each passage focuses on complementary details of the same event.[15]

Final Reflections

As mentioned earlier, that night may be the darkest in human history. Jesus Christ, the Son of God, was betrayed into the hands of sinners. As the events unfold, we see the betrayal of a friend, the leader of the Twelve denying he even knows Jesus, the leaders of the Jewish people frantically searching for false witnesses to agree on charges worthy of death, and Jesus confessing that he is the Son of Man who will be seated at the right hand of the Father. The following discussion will focus on each of these participants.

Sometimes the question is asked, "How are Peter's denials different than Judas's betrayal?" On the surface they may seem similar, but they are very different. Judas was a complex individual. Since he was the treasurer for the apostolic band, we may assume that he displayed some positive characteristics that others recognized. The role of treasurer is not usually given to someone known to be greedy and irresponsible. While ascribing a single reason for Judas's action is difficult, he tells us himself that greed was a significant aspect: "What are you willing to give

---

[15] For a comprehensive discussion of this event see Brown, *Death of the Messiah*, 1:636–60.

me if I hand him over to you?' So they weighed out thirty pieces of silver for him. And from that time he started looking for a good opportunity to betray him" (Matt 26:15–16). The love of money has contributed to the downfall of more than one person, and Judas appears to have fallen victim to it. Paul gave a serious warning to persons whose ambition is to get rich: "But those who want to be rich fall into temptation, a trap, and many foolish and harmful desires, which plunge people into ruin and destruction. For the love of money is a root of all kinds of evil, and by craving it, some have wandered away from the faith and pierced themselves with many griefs" (1 Tim 6:9–10).

Judas's betrayal had a cosmic element as well—he was indwelt by Satan (John 13:27). We can ask how Satan was able to use Judas and eventually indwell him. As noted earlier, Judas was a thief (12:4–6). Prolonged unconfessed and unrepentant sin seems to be the grounds through which Satan entered him. Judas is a painful reminder of how close a person can be to Jesus but not experience saving grace.

In contrast to Judas's scheming, Peter's denials were the result of being overcome by momentary fear for his life. What led to his collapse was the multifaceted convergence of his overconfidence—refusing to listen to Jesus's warning, sleeping instead of praying, and failing to take his own weaknesses seriously. Moreover, Peter also became the focus of satanic attention. Little did he understand, as he warmed himself by the fire in the high priest's courtyard, he was in the process of being sifted. The most important difference between Peter and Judas is while Judas hung himself in remorse, Peter demonstrated repentance by going on to live a life for God's glory and eventually to die a martyr's death (21:18–19).

The religious leaders showed no concern for justice, only for maintaining their positions of power. Their eyes were blinded, as they perceived Jesus to be their enemy, but in fact he was their God. The Sanhedrin demonstrated a cynical, politically savvy, self-serving disposition. They compromised their moral integrity in order to retain positions of power. Whenever someone becomes more concerned about the perks of leadership than the spiritual responsibilities of it, he or she falls prey to the sin of the Sanhedrin. Leadership gone awry is an ugly thing. There comes a point when a person can become blinded to his or her own selfish desires for power. Jesus was correct when he described the scribes and Pharisees as whitewashed tombs. What made this situation even more tragic was they knew the Scriptures better than anyone in the world. This is a strong reminder that we are not what we know, but what we do with that knowledge. May God give his church leaders that do not demonstrate an insatiable hunger for power, but for washing feet!

As we have seen, Caiaphas brought the proceedings to a climactic moment when he pressed the question on Jesus, "Are you the Messiah, the Son of the Blessed One?" (Mark 14:61). If there were any doubts about who Jesus believed himself to be, they were erased in that moment: "'I am,' said Jesus, 'and you will see **the Son of Man seated at the right hand of Power and coming with the clouds of heaven'**" (v. 62). Jesus made absolutely clear he would come again one day. He acknowledged his return to his disciples on the Mount of Olives and now to those who hated him and wanted him executed. Jesus's second coming as the Son of Man should be a strong encouragement to those who are suffering for their faith. There is a better world coming when Jesus returns to reward his people and judge his enemies.

Hymn of Response

When I survey the wondrous cross
On which the Prince of glory died,
My richest gain I count but loss,
And pour contempt on all my pride.

Forbid it, Lord, that I should boast,
Save in the death of Christ, my God;
All the vain things that charm me most,
I sacrifice them to His blood.

See, from His head, His hands, His feet,
Sorrow and love flow mingled down;
Did e'er such love and sorrow meet,
Or thorns compose so rich a crown?

Were the whole realm of nature mine,
That were a present far too small;
Love so amazing, so divine,
Demands my soul, my life, my all![16]

---

[16] Isaac Watts, "When I Survey the Wondrous Cross," 1707, *Baptist Hymnal*, #234, 235.

CHAPTER 8

THE ROMAN TRIAL: GUILTY OF TREASON

FRIDAY: APRIL 7, AD 30

As the sun rose on Friday morning, those who conspired against Jesus had convicted him of blasphemy. Next, they must convince the Roman governor he deserved to die. They would find Pilate much less accommodating than they could have imagined. While all four Gospels describe Jesus before Pontius Pilate, John's Gospel gives the most detail. John mentions Jesus's trial before the Sanhedrin with just a passing reference. His detail about the Roman trial provides insight into the discussions between Jesus and Pilate that are not found in the Synoptics. Just as Jesus's Jewish trial had three phases, so did his Roman trial.

Phase One: Jesus before Pilate[1]

The trial before Pilate, the Roman governor of Judea, began in the early morning hours.[2] Pilate probably thought he could conduct the trial relatively quickly before most of the city even knew Jesus had been arrested. The likely location where Pilate adjudicated Jesus's case was the magnificent palace of Herod the Great, built on the Western Ridge of the upper city. Pilate resided there when he stayed in Jerusalem.[3] His primary residence was Caesarea, but he would come to Jerusalem during the Jewish festivals to make sure there were no disruptions.[4]

The chief priests led Jesus to the praetorium to appear before Pilate. They refused to go inside to avoid defilement and thereby become unable to participate in the other festive meals during the week. Pilate emerged from the praetorium and asked what charges were being brought against Jesus. Three charges were presented: (1) inciting the nation; (2) forbidding the payment of taxes to Caesar; and (3) making himself out to be the Messiah (Luke 23:2). Pilate seemed uninterested in hearing the case and instructed the Jewish leaders to handle the matter themselves. Their response indicates they wanted nothing short of execution, saying, "It's not legal for us to put anyone to death" (John 18:31). The Romans prohibited those

---

[1] Matt 27:2, 11–14; Mark 15:1b–5; Luke 23:1–5; John 18:28–38.

[2] For a better understanding of Pilate, see the discussion by Schnabel, *Jesus in Jerusalem*, 91–94 (see chap. 1, n. 10).

[3] Two less likely locations are Antonia fortress, at the northwest corner of the temple, and the Hasmonaean royal palace on the western slope of the Tyropoeon Valley.

[4] Craig Keener, *John*, Zondervan Illustrated Bible Backgrounds Commentary 2A (Grand Rapids, MI: Zondervan, 2019), 179–80.

they governed to have the power of the sword. This kept those subjugated to them from executing citizens who collaborated with the Romans.[5]

Pilate took Jesus inside the praetorium for a private interrogation (vv. 33–37). Pilate wanted to know more about the third accusation: "Are you the king of the Jews?" Jesus's answer in the Synoptic Gospels seems less than forthcoming: "You say so."[6] Jesus's response, however, likely had to do with the fact that Pilate could not comprehend the kind of king Jesus is. It must have stung Jesus quite a bit for Pilate to mention that his own people handed him over. Jesus's words, "My kingdom is not of this world," surely sounded foolish to Pilate—a kingdom without any physical territory and no military to fight for it.

After further discussion, Pilate announced to the crowd that he found no guilt in Jesus. This is the first of three times Pilate declared Jesus innocent (Luke 23:4; John 18:38). In response, the chief priests began to accuse Jesus harshly. Jesus's silence stunned Pilate because he knew Jesus's life was on the line. When Pilate learned Jesus was from Galilee, he saw a way to avoid having to render a verdict against Jesus—he could send him to Herod Antipas. It is hard to believe Pilate's reluctance to condemn Jesus had anything to do with his being an honorable person. It is far more probable he wanted to find a way to release Jesus out of his disdain for the Jewish leadership. Pilate took the opportunity to send Jesus to Antipas, who was in Jerusalem to celebrate Passover.

---

[5] Stephen's death in Acts 7 should be understood as a spontaneous act of mob violence.

[6] Matt 27:11; Mark 15:2; Luke 23:3.

Phase Two: Jesus before Herod Antipas[7]

Only Luke records Jesus's appearance before Herod Antipas. Antipas was tetrarch over Galilee and Perea from 4 BC to AD 39. He was the son of Herod the Great. Antipas was quite pleased to encounter Jesus. He obviously had heard about Jesus's miracles and hoped to see him perform one. Antipas's interrogation of Jesus did not go well. Jesus's refusal to engage Antipas's questions enraged him. Why did Jesus refuse to speak to him? Earlier in Jesus's ministry, he called Antipas a "fox" (Luke 13:32). Foxes were unclean animals to the Jewish people. While Antipas put on the façade of being a faithful Jew, his behavior revealed otherwise. He had been put in power by Caesar Augustus, the Roman emperor. To honor his Roman overlords, Antipas built a grand new capital city named Tiberias named after the current emperor Tiberius. No record exists of Jesus ever visiting the city. Furthermore, Antipas divorced his first wife, which had been a political union, as she was the daughter of an Arab ruler, to marry Herodias, the wife of his half-brother. Finally, Antipas ordered the decapitation of John the Baptist. John had been a persistent critic of Herod for his dubious marriage. In short, Herod Antipas served as an unsavory and unscrupulous puppet ruler of the Romans. He certainly was not one to trifle with.

While Jesus had every reason to be afraid of Antipas, he refused to speak a word to him. When Antipas recognized that he was getting nowhere and heard the vehement accusations toward Jesus, he and his soldiers began to taunt him. They mocked Jesus, placed a beautiful robe over his shoulders, and then sent him back to Pilate. Luke adds the interesting thought that Herod and Pilate

---

[7] Luke 23:6–12.

became friends that day. We do not know why they had been at odds; it may have been nothing more than two powerful men suspicious of one another, or it may have resulted from Pilate's order to kill some Galileans during a festival in Jerusalem (Luke 13:1).

Phase Three: The Roman Trial: Jesus before Pilate Again[8]

After Antipas finished taunting Jesus, he sent him back to Pilate. As this scene unfolds, it becomes more evident that the chief priests wanted Jesus to die by crucifixion. From a theological position John's Gospel continues to highlight the issue of Jesus's kingship. Pilate was torn between releasing Jesus and placating the chief priests. It becomes abundantly clear that Pilate did not believe Jesus to be guilty of a capital offense. He hoped that by sending him to Antipas he could avoid having to render a verdict.

Another possible avenue for setting Jesus free was the practice of releasing one prisoner during Passover. While no historical documentation outside the Gospels exists for this practice, it is hard to imagine the Evangelists fabricating this kind of story. It makes sense historically as a gesture toward the Jews, since Passover commemorated freedom from bondage. Pilate offered the crowd a choice between Jesus and a man named Barabbas. The Gospel writers identify Barabbas by his crimes—insurrection and murder. He was the very kind of person for which crucifixion was intended. Oddly enough, the name *Barabbas* means "son of abba." Pilate offered the crowd a choice between God's beloved Son and a notorious criminal. Pilate certainly thought the crowd would ask for Jesus's release. He had done nothing that deserved death, but

---

[8] Matt 27:15–26; Mark 15:6–15; Luke 23:13–25; John 18:39–19:16.

Barabbas had committed capital offenses. Pilate knew the Jews had handed over Jesus out of envy (Matt 27:16). Surprisingly, the crowd turned against Jesus. Up to that point, his primary foes had been the religious leaders. Why did the crowds join in turning against him? The early morning hour of these events may indicate that the Sanhedrin gathered most of the crowd, while those who would have come to Jesus's defense were just then rousing after the festivities of the previous night's celebration.

Pilate was momentarily distracted by a message from his wife (v. 19). While Jesus was being betrayed and arrested in the middle of the night, Pilate's wife struggled to sleep, having a nightmare because of "that righteous man." The Romans considered dreams as providing guidance and warnings to those having them. As far as we know, she had never met Jesus, but it is quite possible she had heard about his miracles. While Pilate was distracted with his wife's message, the chief priests were working the crowds, stirring them up to ask for Barabbas. When Pilate returned to the proceedings, he was shocked to hear the crowds cry out, "Barabbas!" He asked them what he was to do with Jesus, "who is called Christ" (v. 20–22). For the first time the crowds utter the word "crucify" (*stauroō*). Pilate protested again, pointing to Jesus's innocence. The crowd cried out all the louder, "Crucify him!" Pilate perceived he might have a riot on his hands and relented to the crowd's demand. Before he did, he washed his hands, indicating his refusal to accept responsibility for the decision (v. 24).[9] The crowd's ominous response is chilling: "His blood be on us on and our children" (v. 25). The reference to "our children" signifies the solidarity of the family. The destruction of the temple in AD 70 was possibly God's judgment on the crowd

---

[9] See also Deut 21:6–8; Pss 26:6; 73:13.

and their children.[10] Many persons have used this verse as an excuse for anti-Semitism; however, we ought to reject the view that all Jewish people for all time are guilty of the death of Jesus, or even all the Jewish people in Jesus's day. Jesus's chief opponents were the Pharisees and the religious leadership in Jerusalem.

John includes a shocking exchange lacking in the Synoptic Gospels between Pilate and the chief priests. As Pilate approached the point of total frustration with the crowd he asked, "Should I crucify your king?" The chief priests responded, "We have no king but Caesar!" (John 19:15). When it came down to Jesus or Caesar, the chief priests chose Caesar.

Another interesting dimension is the choice between Jesus and Barabbas. The leaders chose a bandit over their Messiah. Earlier in his ministry, Jesus referred to the Jewish leaders as "thieves and robbers" (10:8). At the Last Supper, Jesus warned the disciples that the world would love its own (15:19). Now, one who seeks a kingdom "with swords and clubs" goes free, and one who refuses an earthly kingdom is condemned to death.

Final Reflections

The most important truths in this chapter are Christological. Jesus, the Son of God and King of Israel, was condemned to die by crucifixion. We see here the Savior of the world mocked, beaten, and rejected by his own people. He was condemned by a man who believed him to be innocent. The one condemned to death spoke the world into existence and is the object of angelic

---

[10] W. D. Davies and Dale C. Allison Jr., *Matthew 19–28*, The International Critical Commentary on the Holy Scriptures of the Old and New Testament, vol. 3 (New York: T&T Clark, 1997), 591–92.

worship. He fed the hungry, healed the sick, cast out demons, and resuscitated the dead; and still they hated him. He came into this world to save sinners. He did not come to be served but to serve. We should stand (or better, fall on our faces!) in amazement at Jesus's wondrous love. We must never forget, as we consider these events, all that Jesus experienced for our salvation. Before he was even nailed to the cross, he was despised and rejected. The apostle Peter put it this way: "For you were called to this, because Christ also suffered for you, leaving you an example, that you should follow in his steps. He did not commit sin, **and no deceit was found in his mouth;** when he was insulted, he did not insult in return; when he suffered, he did not threaten but entrusted himself to the one who judges justly" (1 Pet 2:21–23).

The fact that the Jewish leaders chose Caesar instead of Jesus as their king is significant. They acknowledged a human power they thought could help them maintain their own status. Instead, Roman power ultimately destroyed Jerusalem and the temple, and it decimated the Jewish people. The next generation paid dearly for the sins of their fathers. Today, people refuse to allow Jesus to be their King for much the same reason; they desire to maintain the status quo in their lives. They make choices based upon short-term goals and personal comfort. The religious leaders experienced the great privilege of hearing Jesus speak and watching him perform miracles, and still they claimed another king besides Jesus. We must never forget the great danger into which a person falls by continually rejecting the Light. There is such a thing as judicial blindness. The words of Proverbs 1:24–26 seem especially appropriate to such a people:

> Since I called out and you refused,
> extended my hand and no one paid attention,

since you neglected all my counsel
and did not accept my correction,
I, in turn, will laugh at your calamity.
I will mock when terror strikes you.

Finally, we should think seriously for a moment about Pilate. Pilate let this unbelievable opportunity slip through his fingers. Three times he pronounced Jesus not guilty (John 18:38; 19:4, 6). He even tried to set Jesus free (19:12). But when courage and honor hung in the balance, Pilate chose political expediency. Under intense pressure we, too, may feel our security threatened. But, unlike Pilate, we must stand for what is true, even if the consequences mean personal loss. If we do not, we will lose something even more valuable—our integrity.

Hymn of Response

Christ stood before Pilate with fettered hands,
And answered not a word;
The throng surged 'round with shouts and jeers,
While Pilate's heart was stirred;
"I find no fault in this Man" he said,
But still the more they cried;
"Away with Him," and on the cross,
The King of glory died.

Refrain:

No fault can I find in Jesus,
The "Man of Calvary;"
O may He find no fault in me,
When His face I see.

Can you say with Pilate, I find no fault,
In Him who went His way;
And spent His life in pointing men
To realms of endless day;
Who healed the sick, yes, and raised the dead,
Who made the blind to see;
And thro' His love for you and me,
Died on the cruel tree.

Refrain:

No fault can I find in Jesus,
The "Man of Calvary;"
O may He find no fault in me,
When His face I see.

No fault can I find with Christ my Lord,
But wonderful to know
That He, who conquered sin and death,
Could ever love me so,
As to bear the shameful and cruel cross,
That I might fully be
Released from sin and dwell with Him,
Thro' all eternity.

Refrain:

No fault can I find in Jesus,
The "Man of Calvary;"
O may He find no fault in me,
When His face I see.[11]

---

[11] Lida Shivers Leech, "No Fault in Him," 1918, *New Songs of Pentecost 3*, #31, Hymnary.org, https://hymnary.org/hymn/NSP31918/31.

CHAPTER 9

THE CRUCIFIXION AND DEATH OF JESUS CHRIST

GOOD FRIDAY: APRIL 7, AD 30

After Pilate condemned Jesus and he was abused by the Roman soldiers, events unfolded quickly.[1] When the four accounts of Jesus's crucifixion are examined side by side, Matthew and Mark are the most similar, while Luke and John are quite unique. We must remember that there are four accounts describing the same event from different vantage points, each focusing on the aspects the author wanted to emphasize to their audience. For example, of the famous "Seven Sayings from the Cross," Matthew and Mark share one, while Luke and John each have three that are distinctive to them. As we turn our attention to the crucifixion, death, and burial of Jesus, we examine Jesus's purpose in coming.

---

[1] Matt 27:31–66; Mark 15:20–47; Luke 23:26–54; John 19:17–42.

Mockery of King Jesus[2]

Jesus was led away to the praetorium. Roman soldiers mocked him, placed a purple robe on him, put a "crown of thorns" on his head, anointed him with their spit, and taunted him by false homage. When they finished, they led him away to crucifixion.

John 19:14 indicates the time Pilate took his seat to make his pronouncement was "about the sixth hour" (noon). Mark 15:25 records the time as "the third hour" (9:00 a.m.). Matthew and Luke do not indicate a time, but they do agree with Mark 15:33 that darkness fell at the sixth hour (twelve noon). The best way to resolve the apparent conflict is to remember that time designations in that day lacked today's exactness. For someone to say it was 9:25 a.m. would be virtually impossible because they did not have clocks in that day. All the New Testament time references—with only three exceptions—are the third, sixth, and ninth hours (9:00 a.m., noon, and 3:00 p.m.).[3] While greater precision was possible, people clearly referred to time in broad terms. Therefore, Jesus was crucified sometime between 9:00 a.m. and noon.

Prior to crucifixion, the Romans flogged their victims. Roman flogging was vastly different than the Jews' thirty-nine lashes. Persons condemned to death were tied to a post and beaten with leather straps that were embedded with sharp pieces of bone and metal.[4] The bone and metal would dig into the victims' back, ripping off flesh and often exposing bone and internal

---

[2] Matt 27:27–31; Mark 15:16–19, 25; John 19:14.
[3] The exceptions are Matt 20:6; John 1:39; 4:52.
[4] Keener, *John*, 190–91 (see chap. 8, n. 4).

organs, with death during flogging not being uncommon. Jesus would have been brutally beaten by his Roman captors.

The Journey to Golgotha[5]

As Jesus was led from the walled city of Jerusalem, he collapsed under the weight of the horizontal beam (*patibulum*). Normally men condemned to death were forced to carry the crossbeam, weighing thirty to forty pounds, to the place of crucifixion. The vertical post (*staticulum*) was left in the ground as a warning to those considering rebellion against Roman authority. Since Jesus was physically unable to carry his crossbeam to the site of crucifixion, the Romans conscripted Simon of Cyrene into service. John's Gospel does not include the role of Simon.

Simon was probably visiting Jerusalem to celebrate Passover. Cyrene was an important city of Libya in North Africa with a large Jewish population. Mark's Gospel makes a parenthetical reference to Simon's sons, Alexander and Rufus (15:21). The sons are referred to in a way that suggests Mark's readers knew them. Rufus may be the same person referred to in Rom 16:13. If these references are to the same Rufus, then the two boys and their father likely became followers of Jesus because of this "chance" encounter.

As Jesus journeyed to the site of execution, he paused momentarily to interact with the "daughters of Jerusalem"

---

[5] Matt 27:31–34; Mark 15:20–23; Luke 23:26–33; John 19:17. The classic work on crucifixion is Martin Hengel, *Crucifixion in the Ancient World* (Philadelphia: Fortress, 1977). For a more up-to-date and succinct discussion, see John A. Dennis, "Death of Jesus," in Green, *Dictionary of Jesus and the Gospels*, 2nd ed., 172–93 (see chap. 1, n. 2).

(Luke 23:26–31). Only Luke describes this conversation. The women were mourning over what was taking place. Jesus warned them of what lay ahead for them and prophesies the future destruction of the city by the Romans. Jesus encouraged them not to cry for him but for themselves and their children. What they would experience was the complete destruction of the city and all those within its walls.

The First Three Hours of Crucifixion[6]

The site of execution was called Golgotha, an Aramaic word, meaning "place of the skull," although why the site was known by this name is disputed. The reason may have been because the site itself was a hill shaped like a skull. Another possible reason may be the fact that the site was a place of suffering and death. The Latin Vulgate translates "skull" as *calvariae*, from which we get the word *Calvary*. At the time of Jesus's crucifixion, the site was outside the city walls. But when the city was enlarged, Golgotha was enclosed within the third wall.[7]

After arriving at the site, Jesus was offered wine mixed with myrrh. Myrrh is a spice derived from plants native to the Arabian Desert and parts of Africa. Matthew refers to it as "vinegar" or "gall" (Matt 27:34). We cannot know if the offer was an expression of kindness or taunting. Either way, Jesus rejected the offer. The passage may be an allusion to Psalm 69:21:

---

[6] Matt 27:35–44; Mark 15:24–32; Luke 23:33b–43; John 19:18–27.

[7] Most scholars seem to agree that the site of Jesus's crucifixion and burial is located at the site currently occupied by the Church of the Holy Sepulchre. For a recent discussion on Golgotha and Jesus's tomb, see Schnabel, *Jesus in Jerusalem*, 132–37 (see chap. 1, n. 10).

Instead, they gave me gall for my food,
and for my thirst
they gave me vinegar to drink.

The "invention" of crucifixion is attributed to the Medes and Persians. The practice spread throughout the Mediterranean world through the conquest of Alexander the Great. The Romans, however, "perfected" the horrific form of execution. Crucifixion remained the major form of capital punishment in the Roman Empire until it was outlawed by Constantine in AD 337.

The Gospel writers add none of the gruesome details that one would have seen at a crucifixion. A victim was nailed or tied to a cross. Those who were nailed had heavy wrought iron nails driven through the wrists. The ankles would be attached similarly to the vertical wooden beam. Victims often languished for several days. During that time they were susceptible to the pecking of birds and the horror of wild dogs and insects. To add to the horrific nature of the torment, victims were normally crucified naked. Occasionally, the Romans allowed Jewish victims to wear a loincloth, which was the exception rather than the rule. If the victim lingered too long, death was hastened by the breaking of the legs. To prevent a premature death by asphyxiation, a small seat or footrest would be placed on the vertical beam to extend the torment. Crosses were occasionally X-shaped but usually resembled either a capital *T* or lowercase *t* in form. The latter is more likely in Jesus's case due to the placing of a placard over his head.

Jesus's opponents understood his death on the cross to indicate he was cursed by God. Deut 21:22–23 reads,

If anyone is found guilty of an offense deserving the death penalty and is executed, and you hang his body on

a tree, you are not to leave his corpse on the tree over-
night but are to bury him that day, for anyone hung on
a tree is under God's curse. You must not defile the land
the LORD your God is giving you as an inheritance.

Two criminals (*lēstēs*) were crucified with Jesus.[8] Since Jesus
was the more prominent person he was placed in the middle.
The two criminals were likely comrades of Barabbas. The fact
that Jesus died between two criminals is reminiscent of Isa 53:12
which reads,

> Therefore I will give him the many as a portion,
> and he will receive the mighty as spoil,
> because he willingly submitted to death,
> and was counted among the rebels;
> yet he bore the sin of many
> and interceded for the rebels.

One of the "benefits" of being on detail at a crucifixion was
the opportunity to secure a portion of the victims' possessions.[9]
All four Gospels describe the soldiers dividing Jesus's clothes by
casting lots. Only John describes Jesus's seamless garment not
being divided,[10] which John connects directly to Ps 22:18. This

---

[8] Matt 27:38; Mark 15:27; Luke 23:33.

[9] Matt 27:35; Mark 15:24; Luke 23:34; John 19:23–24.

[10] John's purpose in recounting this event has been debated. Some
believe John may be recalling the vestments of the high priest (Exod 28;
39:27–29; Lev 16:4). Yet there is no mention in the Old Testament of them
being seamless (this detail is referred to by Josephus [*Antiquities* 3.7.16]).
In addition, while John clearly exploits Passover symbolism, he does not
interpret Jesus's death or ministry against a priestly background.

Psalm plays an important role in the description of Jesus's crucifixion: "They divided my garments among themselves, / and they cast lots for my clothing." What an amazing contrast between the kingdom of the world and the kingdom of God. While Jesus suffered for the sins of humankind, the soldiers played games for his few possessions.

Jesus's seven sayings from the cross are some of the most precious words in the Bible. I have included a chart below with cross-references to enable you to better understand Jesus's statements and their implications. Each of the seven statements are commented on after the chart.

Saying	Cross-Reference
Luke 23:34—Then Jesus said, "Father, forgive them, because they do not know what they are doing." And they divided his clothes and cast lots.	Luke 6:29, 35—If anyone hits you on the cheek, offer the other also. And if anyone takes away your coat, don't hold back your shirt either. . . . But love your enemies, do what is good, and lend, expecting nothing in return. Then your reward will be great, and you will be children of the Most High. For he is gracious to the ungrateful and evil. Acts 7:54–60—When they heard these things, they were enraged and gnashed their teeth at him. Stephen, full of the Holy Spirit, gazed into heaven. He saw the glory of God, and Jesus standing at the right hand of God. He said, "Look, I see the heavens opened and the Son of Man standing at the right hand of God!"

	They yelled at the top of their voices, covered their ears, and together rushed against him. They dragged him out of the city and began to stone him. And the witnesses laid their garments at the feet of a young man named Saul. While they were stoning Stephen, he called out, "Lord Jesus, receive my spirit!" He knelt down and cried out with a loud voice, "Lord, do not hold this sin against them!" And after saying this, he fell asleep.
	1 Cor 2:6–8—We do, however, speak a wisdom among the mature, but not a wisdom of this age, or of the rulers of this age, who are coming to nothing. On the contrary, we speak God's hidden wisdom in a mystery, a wisdom God predestined before the ages for our glory. None of the rulers of this age knew this wisdom, because if they had known it, they would not have crucified the Lord of glory.
John 19:26–27—When Jesus saw his mother and the disciple he loved standing there, he said to his mother, "Woman, here is your son." Then he said to the disciple, "Here is your mother." And from that hour the disciple took her into his home.	**Exod 20:12**—Honor your father and your mother so that you may have a long life in the land that the LORD your God is giving you. **Eph 6:2–3—Honor your father and mother**, which is the first commandment with a promise, **so that it may go well with you and that you may have a long life in the land**.

Luke 23:43—And he said to him, "Truly I tell you, today you will be with me in paradise."	**2 Cor 12:4**—[This man] was caught up into paradise and heard inexpressible words, which a human being is not allowed to speak. **Rev 2:7**—Let anyone who has ears to hear listen to what the Spirit says to the churches. To the one who conquers, I will give the right to eat from the tree of life, which is in the paradise of God.
Mark 15:34—And at three Jesus cried out with a loud voice, *"Eloi, Eloi, lemá sabachthání?"* which is translated, "My God, my God, why have you abandoned me?" **Matt 27:46**—About three in the afternoon Jesus cried out with a loud voice, *"Elí, Elí, lemá sabachthání?"* that is, "My God, my God, why have you abandoned me?"	**Ps 22:1**—My God, my God, why have you abandoned me? / Why are you so far from my deliverance / and from my words of groaning?
John 19:28—After this, when Jesus knew that everything was now finished that the Scripture might be fulfilled, he said, "I'm thirsty."	**Ps 22:15**—My strength is dried up like baked clay; / my tongue sticks to the roof of my mouth. / You put me into the dust of death. **Ps 69:21**—Instead, they gave me gall for my food, / and for my thirst / they gave me vinegar to drink.

John 19:30—When Jesus had received the sour wine, he said, "It is finished." Then bowing his head, he gave up his spirit.	**Luke 12:50**—But I have a baptism to undergo, and how it consumes me until it is finished! **John 4:34**—"My food is to do the will of him who sent me and to finish his work," Jesus told them. **John 17:4**—I have glorified you on the earth by completing the work you gave me to do. **John 19:28**—After this, when Jesus knew that everything was now finished that the Scripture might be fulfilled, he said, "I'm thirsty."
Luke 23:46—And Jesus called out with a loud voice, "Father, **into your hands I entrust my spirit**." Saying this, he breathed his last.	**Ps 31:5**—Into your hand I entrust my spirit; / you have redeemed me, LORD, God of truth. **Isa 53:12**—Therefore I will give him the many as a portion, and he will receive the mighty as spoil, because he willingly submitted to death, and was counted among the rebels; yet he bore the sin of many and interceded for the rebels. **John 19:30**—When Jesus had received the sour wine, he said, "It is finished." Then bowing his head, he gave up his spirit. **1 Cor 15:55**—**Where, death, is your victory? / Where, death, is your sting?** **1 Pet 4:19**—So then, let those who suffer according to God's will entrust themselves to a faithful Creator while doing what is good.

Jesus's first words from the cross were a prayer of forgiveness: "Father, forgive them, because they do not know what they are doing" (Luke 23:34). Jesus put his own teaching into practice in this most dire of moments. He taught his disciples to love their enemies and to pray for them (6:28). He became an example for all believers who suffer for their faith (Acts 7:60; 1 Pet 2:21–24). Jesus's prayer did not absolve those responsible for his crucifixion of all their sins but was a prayer that they be not held accountable for the sin of killing God's Son. Paul expressed the idea this way to the Corinthians: "None of the rulers of this age knew this wisdom, because if they had known it, they would not have crucified the Lord of glory" (1 Cor 2:8).

John reports the chief priests' objection to the wording of the placard placed over Jesus's head (John 19:19–22). The placard read, "JESUS OF NAZARETH, THE KING OF THE JEWS." The chief priests found the placard insulting and demanded it be changed to read, "He said 'I am the King of the Jews.'" Pilate's intention in stating the wording as he did would have been to humiliate both Jesus and the religious leaders. The wording was written in Aramaic, Latin, and Greek (v. 20). Aramaic was the language of the Jewish people, Latin the language of the Roman government, and Greek the street language of the empire. Ironically, what Pilate meant as an insult to Jesus could not have been truer.

Several of Jesus's female followers watched in horror from a distance, while a few others stood close to the cross, including Mary, Jesus's mother.[11] In a very touching exchange, Jesus entrusted his mother's care into the hands of the beloved

---

[11] Harmonization of the list of female names at the crucifixion and tomb is challenging. For a detailed examination see Brown, *Death of the Messiah*, 2:1013–19 (see chap. 7, n. 3). A comparison of the Gospels suggests the presence of Mary the mother of Jesus; Mary the wife of Clopas and mother of James the Younger and Joseph; Salome the sister of Jesus's mother as well as wife of Zebedee and mother of James and John; Mary

disciple (John). We may wonder why John includes this emotional exchange (vv. 25–27). Whatever his purpose, we see a shining example of Jesus's tender love for his mother. As he suffered, struggling for every breath, he focused on others. Jesus likely entrusted his mother's care to John to ensure her safety in a volatile situation.[12] One may also wonder whether the words spoken by Simeon when Jesus was an infant came to her mind in those moments: "Indeed, this child is destined to cause the fall and rise of many in Israel and to be a sign that will be opposed—and a sword will pierce your own soul—that the thoughts of many hearts may be revealed" (Luke 2:34–35).

Jesus was taunted and mocked from all sides—those passing by the religious leaders, Roman soldiers, and even the two dying criminals. Those passing by are described as yelling insults (*blasphēmeō*) and shaking their heads at him as a sign of contempt.[13] The accusation that Jesus supposedly threatened the temple was raised; and the taunt "Save yourself," which became a repeated theme, was spoken for the first time. The irony is the only way Jesus could save others was by not saving himself.

The chief priests and the scribes joined in the mocking, taunting Jesus to come down from the cross and "save himself" as he "saved others" (Matt 27:42). The chief priests' coldheartedness is on full display here. Rather than gloat from a distance, they

---

Magdalene; and Joanna (at the tomb in Luke). See Matt 27:55–56; Mark 15:40–41; Luke 23:49; and John 19:25.

[12] John 19:25 is the only reference in the New Testament to Jesus's aunt. She may have been the wife of Zebedee (Salome), the mother of James and John, making Jesus and John the apostle cousins. Mary (the wife of Clopas) is mentioned directly only here. Mary Magdalene is present both at the cross and the empty tomb (John 20:1).

[13] Matt 27:39–40; Mark 15:29–30. Also see Ps 22:7; Lam 2:15.

came near the cross to revel in their supposed victory over the Galilean carpenter. Even the soldiers, who gambled for Jesus's possessions, could not help but participate in the celebration. They offered Jesus sour wine to drink—whether as an act of kindness or a form of taunting is unclear (Luke 23:36).

The criminals hanging on either side of Jesus even mustered the strength to add their insults. One would think that as the two criminals fought for every breath, they would not expend the strength to join in the mocking.[14] At some point one of the two criminals came to his senses. He began to rebuke his fellow prisoner for mocking Jesus (v. 40). The conversion of this "thief on the cross" reminds us of Jesus's power to save. We do not know what happened to change his mind, except God's grace was at work in him. He went from taunting Jesus to defending him and asking Jesus to remember him when he came into his kingdom. While the words "faith" and "repentance" do not appear, they are evident in the man's heart by his words.

After the thief rebuked his fellow criminal, he acknowledged they were receiving what they deserved for their crimes, but Jesus had done nothing wrong (v. 41). This acknowledgment of Jesus's innocence was added to the earlier pronouncements by Pilate and Antipas. We hear his words of faith in the simple request, "Remember me when you come into your kingdom" (v. 42). Amazing! When this criminal looked at Jesus, he saw a king. His only request was for King Jesus to remember him when he entered his kingdom. The salvation of the thief on the cross is a reminder of the depth of God's grace. Jesus's response was brief: "Today you will be with me in paradise" (v. 43), Paradise (*paradeisos*) is another name for heaven, the dwelling place of God, the

---

[14] Luke 23:39; see Matt 27:44; Mark 15:32.

eternal home of the righteous.[15] The Septuagint uses the same Greek word to refer to the garden of Eden (Gen 2:8–9). Jesus's words suggest the restoration of the close communion between God and Adam and Eve prior to the fall.

The Final Three Hours of Crucifixion[16]

At this point Mark supplies another time indicator as darkness descended on the land from the sixth (noon) until the ninth hour (3:00 p.m.).[17] Darkness can represent lament and divine judgment. Jesus's death even had cosmic consequences. The prophet Amos said:

> And in that day—
>   this is the declaration of the Lord GOD—
> I will make the sun go down at noon;
> I will darken the land in the daytime.
> I will turn your feasts into mourning
> and all your songs into lamentation;
> I will cause everyone to wear sackcloth
> and every head to be shaved.
> I will make that grief
> like mourning for an only son
> and its outcome like a bitter day. (Amos 8:9–10)

And Exod 10:22 reads,

---

[15] See 2 Cor 12:3–4; Rev 2:7.

[16] Matt 27:45–50; Mark 15:33–37; Luke 23:44–46; John 19:28–30.

[17] Matt 27:45; Mark 15:33–34; Luke 23:44. Josephus said the ninth hour was the time of the evening sacrifice (*Antiquities* 14.65).

So Moses stretched out his hand toward heaven, and there was thick darkness throughout the land of Egypt for three days.

During the darkness, Jesus cried out with a sense of abandonment (Matt 27:46; Mark 15:34). Mark quotes the Aramaic, *"Eloi, Eloi, lemá sabachtháni?"* which he translates for his readers, "My God, my God, why have you abandoned me?" Matthew quotes the Hebrew equivalent *Eli*. Jesus's words refer to the opening line of Psalm 22, which is a lament psalm that portrays the desolation of the suffering of the righteous one (vv. 1–21) and the eventual triumphant vindication of this one by God (vv. 22–31). These are Jesus' only words from the cross in Mark and Matthew's Gospels. Abandoned by friends, mocked, tormented by his own religious leaders, and surrounded by thieves, Jesus cried out to God. Even these words are misunderstood and mocked by his enemies.

Scholars debate as to whether Jesus's cry of abandonment is an expression of desolation, faith, despair, or trust. Both can be true. Psalm 22 begins with despair but ends with victory. As for Jesus's sense of desolation, Isa 59:1–2 comes to mind:

Indeed, the LORD's arm is not too weak to save,
and his ear is not too deaf to hear.
But your iniquities are separating you
from your God,
and your sins have hidden his face from you
so that he does not listen.

Yet, in quoting Ps 22:1, Jesus also had in mind verses 22–31, which move to a declaration of victory. Even the opening words, "My God, my God" are an expression of faith, evidenced by the personal pronoun. Jesus never forgot that his death was the purpose of his coming. These words are intensely deep and mysterious. As Jesus bore the sins of humanity there was a very real sense in which he had to be cut off from the intimate fellowship and manifest presence of the Father. Jesus's consideration of this moment is what caused his agony in Gethsemane. Passages such as the following reveal something of what was taking place in those hours of darkness.

> We all went astray like sheep;
> we all have turned to our own way;
> and the LORD has punished him
> for the iniquity of us all. . . .
> Yet the LORD was pleased to crush him severely.
> When you make him a guilt offering,
> he will see his seed, he will prolong his days,
> and by his hand, the LORD's pleasure will be accomplished. (Isa 53:6, 10)

> Your eyes are too pure to look on evil,
> and you cannot tolerate wrongdoing.
> So why do you tolerate those who are treacherous?
> Why are you silent
> while one who is wicked swallows up
> one who is more righteous than himself? (Hab 1:13)

> God presented him as the mercy seat by his blood, through faith, to demonstrate his righteousness, because in his restraint God passed over the sins previously committed. (Rom 3:25)

> He made the one who did not know sin to be sin for us, so that in him we might become the righteousness of God. (2 Cor 5:21)

Christ redeemed us from the curse of the law by becoming a curse for us, because it is written, **Cursed is everyone who is hung on a tree.** (Gal 3:13)

These verses and many others like them reveal the price Jesus paid to redeem sinful humanity.

When Jesus said in John 19:28, "I'm thirsty" (*dipsaō*), he no doubt was speaking quite literally. But his words also are an allusion to either Ps 22:15 ("My tongue sticks to the roof of my mouth") or, more likely, an allusion to Ps 69:21 ("They gave me vinegar to drink"). In response, a bystander offered a sponge soaked in wine and Jesus drank from it. Scripture was being fulfilled down to the smallest of details.

The taste of the wine strengthened Jesus physically, and in John 19:30 he cried out, "It is finished" (*teleō*). Mission accomplished! He completed the work his Father gave him to do.[18] He bore the sins of humankind in his body and suffered God's wrath to redeem a people for his own possession. Jesus then cried out, "Father, **into your hands I entrust my spirit**" (Luke 23:46). His final words are a prayer of the commitment of his spirit into the hands of his heavenly Father. Earlier, he cried out, "My God, my God"; here he returned to the term of endearment, "Father."

Events Accompanying Jesus's Death[19]

Several events having theological significance took place as Jesus died. First, the curtain of the temple in Jerusalem was torn in

---

[18] See John 4:34; 17:4.

[19] Matt 27:51–56; Mark 15:38–41; Luke 23:45–49; John 19:31–38.

two.[20] We cannot know with certainty which curtain is being referred to here. One curtain separated the sanctuary from the courtyard, and the other curtain separated the most holy place from the rest of the sanctuary. If the curtain is the former, the tearing (like the darkness) was visible to people. The meaning would then be a foreshadowing of the destruction of the temple. If the curtain was the interior curtain, then the tearing is a sign pointing to the believer's access to God promised in the new covenant (Heb 6:19–20; 9:3–14; 10:19–20). The fact that the curtain was torn from top to bottom suggests God tore it. The referenced curtain more likely refers to the inner curtain, considering the passages in Hebrews.

Matthew describes an earthquake, the splitting of rocks, and the opening of tombs (Matt 27:51–52). This is one of the most difficult passages in the New Testament. The grammar in the Greek suggests that those who were raised were raised after Jesus's resurrection from the dead.[21] Many mysteries remain: Who were these people? Why did God select them to be raised along with Jesus? To whom did they appear? The main point in this event may be found in Paul's statement to the Corinthians, "But as it is, Christ has been raised from the dead, the firstfruits of those who have fallen asleep" (1 Cor 15:20).

While these events were taking place, a Roman centurion who watched as Jesus took his final breath confessed him to be the Son of God.[22] The centurion would have been a part of

---

[20] Matt 27:51; Mark 15:38; Luke 23:45.

[21] For a more complete discussion see Blomberg, *Matthew*, 421 (see chap. 2, n. 4); Michael J. Wilkins, *Matthew*, The NIV Application Commentary (Grand Rapids, MI: Zondervan, 2004), 905–7.

[22] Matt 27:54; Mark 15:39; Luke 23:47.

the detachment deployed at the crucifixion site to keep order. Jesus was likely not the first person the centurion had seen die, although no one ever died as Jesus died. What he witnessed during those hours included: Jesus's prayer for his enemies; his self-control as his opponents taunted him; the exchange between Jesus and the repentant thief; the supernatural darkness; Jesus's cry of abandonment; his prayer of committal of his life into the Father's hands; and his final breath. All these events, and more, moved this battle-tested warrior to make this dramatic confession. While his confession was likely not a trinitarian affirmation of Jesus's deity, it was nonetheless a powerful confession. The readers of the Gospels, however, understand the depth of the confession better than the centurion did.

Witnesses to Jesus's execution returned to their homes mourning this miscarriage of justice (Luke 23:48). Anyone fully aware of the events knew Jesus did not deserve to die. On the one hand, the chief priests' envy, Judas's greed, and Pilate's cowardice led to his execution. On the other hand, Jesus had to die to pay the penalty for humankind's sins. Those who believed Jesus to be the Messiah watched in stunned horror and silence. The prophet from Galilee was dead.

Confirmation of Death[23]

Because the day was the preparation day before the high Sabbath of the Passover, the chief priests requested that Pilate have the legs of the three crucified men broken so they could die and not be left hanging on the cross on the Sabbath. Pilate consented and gave the order. The legs of those hanging on either side of

---

[23] Matt 27:57–58; Mark 15:42–45; Luke 23:50–52; John 19:31–37.

Jesus were broken first. When it was discovered that Jesus was already dead, a soldier pierced his side with the spear. Whether the soldier pierced Jesus's side to make sure he was dead, or out of spite, is impossible to know. John indicates that Jesus's legs not being broken and the piercing of his side fulfill the Scripture:

> [The Passover] is to be eaten in one house. You may not take any of the meat outside the house, and you may not break any of its bones. (Exod 12:46)

> Then I will pour out a spirit of grace and prayer on the house of David and the residents of Jerusalem, and they will look at me whom they pierced. They will mourn for him as one mourns for an only child and weep bitterly for him as one weeps for a firstborn. (Zech 12:10)

The Burial of Jesus's Body and Securing of the Tomb[24]

Joseph of Arimathea stepped into the story from out of the darkness. His courage was demonstrated by asking Pilate for the body of a man condemned by the Romans to death. He not only had to consider what the Romans would think but the chief priests as well. The Sanhedrin would not have been happy with one of their own giving Jesus's body an honorable burial. Pilate granted him permission to take Jesus's body for burial.[25] John indicates that Joseph and Nicodemus prepared Jesus's body for burial and laid it in Joseph's new tomb as a group of women watched.

---

[24] Matt 27:59–66; Mark 15:46–47; Luke 23:53–56; John 19:39–42.

[25] On the burial of Jesus's body, see David W. Chapman, "Burial of Jesus," in Green, *Dictionary of Jesus and the Gospels*, 2nd ed., 97–100 (see chap. 1, n. 2).

Only Matthew recounts the chief priests and Pharisees' request to Pilate to secure Jesus's tomb (Matt 27:62–66). This scene helps prepare the way for the later collaboration of the guards and religious leaders to concoct the lie that the disciples stole Jesus's body (Matt 28:11–15). Jesus's enemies remembered his statement that he would be raised from the dead on the third day, even though they clearly did not believe it. In contrast, Jesus's disciples either did not remember he said he would rise on the third day or did not believe it.

Final Reflections

Jesus's seven sayings from the cross have always been precious to believers. These seven sayings encapsulate much of what Jesus accomplished on our behalf.[26] I will focus my reflections on the first saying: "Father, forgive them, because they do not know what they are doing" (Luke 23:34).[27] The words of Jesus's prayer include passersby who shook their heads in disgust at him; the Roman soldiers who taunted him; the chief priests who stood near the cross mocking him; Pilate, who convicted him of treason; the religious leaders who condemned him for blasphemy; and the criminals on either side of him. As mentioned, Jesus's prayer was not to absolve them of all their sins but for the fact they did not understand they were killing the "Holy and Righteous One" (Acts 3:14).

---

[26] For a comprehensive treatment on the cross, see the classic work by John R. W. Stott, *The Cross of Christ* (Downers Grove, IL: InterVarsity, 1986).

[27] Scholarship is divided on the authenticity of this statement. The words are missing in some of the early Greek manuscripts. One reason I favor its inclusion is because of a similar statement made by Stephen at his martyrdom in the book of Acts. Scholars recognize the fact that Luke carries over many of his themes from his Gospel into Acts.

Jesus's prayer must have made a big impression on the early church. Stephen, the first Christian martyr, prayed a similar prayer as he was being stoned. Luke described the scene this way: "While they were stoning Stephen, he called out, 'Lord Jesus, receive my spirit!' He knelt down and cried out with a loud voice, 'Lord, do not hold this sin against them!' And after saying this, he fell asleep" (Acts 7:59–60). Stephen died as Jesus died, without bitterness and ill-will toward those who killed him. Peter made a similar point: "For you were called to this, because Christ also suffered for you, leaving you an example, that you should follow in his steps. He did not commit sin, **and no deceit was found in his mouth;** when he was insulted, he did not insult in return; when he suffered, he did not threaten but entrusted himself to the one who judges justly" (1 Pet 2:21–23). Jesus taught us not only how to live for God's glory (Stephen), but also how to die for God's glory.

Jesus's death redeems us from sin and empowers us in our sanctification. We live in a fallen world, and almost daily we are tempted to become embittered or resentful toward others because of how we are treated. On our own strength we are unable to respond as Jesus responded. He has not left us on our own, but he has provided the Holy Spirit to strengthen us against sinful responses. Bitterness is an affront to the cross of Christ.

Hymn of Response

There is a fountain filled with blood
Drawn from Immanuel's veins;
And sinners, plunged beneath that flood,
Lose all their guilty stains:
Lose all their guilty stains,
Lose all their guilty stains;

And sinners, plunged beneath that flood,
Lose all their guilty stains.

The dying thief rejoiced to see
That fountain in his day;
And there may I, though vile as he,
Wash all my sins away:
Wash all my sins away,
Wash all my sins away;
And there may I, though vile as he,
Wash all my sins away.

Dear dying Lamb, Thy precious blood
Shall never lose its power
Till all the ransomed church of God
Be saved, to sin no more:
Be saved, to sin no more,
Be saved, to sin no more;
Till all the ransomed church of God
Be saved, to sin no more.

E'er since by faith I saw the stream
Thy flowing wounds supply,
Redeeming love has been my theme,
And shall be till I die:
And shall be till I die,
And shall be till I die;
Redeeming love has been my theme,
And shall be till I die.[28]

---

[28] William Cowper, "There is a Fountain Filled with Blood," 1772, *Baptist Hymnal*, #224.

CHAPTER 10

THE RESURRECTION OF JESUS CHRIST

SUNDAY, APRIL 9, AD 30

The resurrection narratives in the Gospels offer both compelling evidence for the historicity of Jesus's bodily resurrection from the dead and inspiring instructions on its implication for believers.[1] Once again, we will see that the four Gospels offer complementary presentations of the resurrection events, rather than merely repeating an "official transcript" of what transpired. Each account emphasizes what the Evangelists felt to be most important for their readers, which can be seen even in the length of the various accounts.[2]

---

[1] Matt 28:1–20; Mark 16:1–8; Luke 24:1–53; John 20:1–21:25.

[2] Michael R. Licona, *The Resurrection of Jesus: A New Historiographical Approach* (Downers Grove, IL: IVP Academic, 2010); N. T. Wright, *The Resurrection of the Son of God*, Christian Origins and the Question of God 3 (Minneapolis: Fortress, 2003). For a more accessible discussion, see Gary R. Habermas and Michael R. Licona, *The Case for the Resurrection of Jesus* (Grand Rapids, MI: Kregel, 2004), and George Eldon Ladd, *I Believe in the Resurrection of Jesus* (Grand Rapids, MI: Eerdmans, 1975).

Mark's account of the resurrection, for example, is only eight verses long and highlights the women's discovery of the empty tomb and the angelic announcement. Matthew's Gospel, on the other hand, focuses twenty verses on the resurrection and describes only one appearance by Jesus in Jerusalem—to a group of women fleeing the empty tomb. The only other resurrection appearance in Matthew takes place in Galilee, where he gives the famous "Great Commission" to the disciples. Luke's account is fifty-three verses long with no description of resurrection appearances outside Jerusalem, except for two disciples on the road to Emmaus. One could get the impression by reading only Luke's account that the ascension took place on the same day as the resurrection. The book of Acts, however, helps readers to understand that Jesus appeared to his followers over a period of forty days (1:3). The two most important elements in Luke's resurrection account are the physicality of Jesus's resurrection and how his death and resurrection fulfilled Scripture. John's account is the longest, spanning two chapters and fifty-six verses. John describes a series of resurrection appearances in both Jerusalem and Galilee. Much more could be said about each Gospel's presentation, which will be examined in the following discussion.

The hours between Jesus's death and the announcement of his resurrection must have been the darkest in his followers' lives. All their hopes and dreams died when Jesus died. The disciples remained in hiding in or near Jerusalem, fearing for their lives.

The Empty Tomb

When the Sabbath ended on Saturday evening, the shops reopened, giving the women opportunity to purchase spices to anoint Jesus's body. Early Sunday morning they made their way to the tomb, not to embalm Jesus's body but to mitigate the stench of decomposition. Out of love and devotion they wanted to ensure his body received an honorable burial. Why would they anoint Jesus's corpse after the burial by Joseph and Nicodemus? The answer may be nothing more than their love for Jesus and a desire to assuage their grief. The fact that they intended to anoint his body reveals they had no expectation that Jesus would be alive.

The Tomb Visited by Several Women[3]

Matthew recounts an earthquake happened as the women were arriving at the tomb on Sunday morning. The exact timing of the earthquake and the appearance of the angels in relation to it is difficult to unravel, but the two events probably happened some-what simultaneously. According to Matthew, an angel "rolled back the large stone" that secured the tomb (Matt 28:1–2). The stone was not moved to let Jesus out of the tomb but rather to let the women in. The description of the angel(s) is one of splendor and grandeur, not unlike other descriptions of angelic beings in the Bible: "His appearance was like lightning, and his clothing was as white as snow" (v. 3).

The appearance of angels so shocked the Roman sol-diers "they became like dead men" (v. 4). These soldiers had been sent to secure the tomb by order of Pontius Pilate, at the request of the religious leaders. They feared the disciples might attempt to steal Jesus's body and propagate a lie that he had been raised from the dead. Although these soldiers were likely battle-tested fighters, they had never encountered anything

---

[3] Matt 28:1–8, 11–15; Mark 16:1–8; Luke 24:1–8; John 20:1.

like the fierce appearance of the angels. The soldiers fled the scene before the women's arrival. The women would not have been aware of the guards since they were stationed there on the Sabbath. After fleeing the tomb, the guards conspired with the Sanhedrin to concoct a lie accusing the disciples of stealing Jesus's body (vv. 11–15).

Understanding the comings and goings of the women to the tomb that morning is difficult.[4] The women encountered two angels (Matt 28:2–8). They were frightened, and right-fully so! At this point, Mary Magdalene may have left to report the empty tomb to Peter and John (John 20:2–8). The other women were the first to hear the good news that Jesus had been raised from the dead. The angel invited them to examine the empty tomb and reminded them that Jesus told them he would be raised from the dead, "just as he said" (Matt 28:6). He then commanded them to go and tell the disciples Jesus would meet them in Galilee. The women left the tomb with a mixture of fear, astonishment, and joy. They did not say anything to anyone as they made their way to the disciples (Mark 16:8).

Peter and John Race to the Tomb[5]

Mary Magdalene had reported to Peter and John the removal of the stone and the likely taking of Jesus's body (John 20:2). We do not know where the two disciples were staying. They may have been in the upper room, in another safe location in the city, or

---

[4] For a possible explanation, see John Wenham, *The Easter Enigma: Are the Resurrection Accounts in Conflict?* (Grand Rapids, MI: Zondervan, 1984), 76–89.

[5] John 20:2–9.

they may have returned to Bethany. Regardless of their location, they responded to Mary by racing to the tomb. John arrived first, with Peter following shortly behind. John was hesitant to enter the tomb; instead, he stooped down (the opening would have been approximately three feet high)[6] and saw "the linen cloths lying there." If grave robbers had stolen the body, they would never have left the expensive wrappings.

Peter rushed right past John and entered the tomb. He saw not only the linen wrappings, but also "the wrapping that had been on his head [which] was not lying with the linen cloths but was folded up in a separate place by itself" (v. 7). Such graphic detail not only points to an eyewitness reminiscence but also John's emphasis on the scene. The grave clothes appeared to have been in the same position on the burial shelf as when Jesus's body was lying there. The orderliness of the scene suggests Jesus came to life and his body passed through the grave clothes. The entire scene argues against grave robbers.

After John joined Peter in the tomb, what John saw convinced him Jesus must be alive—he "went in, saw, and believed" (v. 8). Some suggest that John believed Mary's report that the tomb was empty and Jesus's body had been taken. John, however, believed Jesus to be alive, although he did not yet understand it from the Scriptures. Peter apparently returned confused and puzzled (Luke 24:12). We are not told why John did not share his belief with Peter or Mary. A possible reason for his silence might be he was stunned and somewhat awestruck.

---

[6] On Jesus's tomb, see Joel B. Green, "The Burial of Jesus," in Green, McKnight, and Marshall, *Dictionary of Jesus and the Gospels*, 88–92 (see chap. 1, n. 16).

Resurrection Appearances

On Resurrection Sunday, Jesus made numerous appearances to his followers. Except for Jesus's journey to Emmaus with two of his followers, all the appearances took place in the city of Jerusalem.[7]

Jesus Appears to Mary Magdalene[8]

Mary Magdalene's encounter with Jesus is one of the most beautiful stories in the Bible. Luke describes how Mary had once been possessed by seven demons (Luke 8:2). Her life must have been a terrible nightmare until she met Jesus. That Sunday morning, she still had no idea that Jesus was alive. As she stooped to look inside the tomb, she encountered two angels. The description of the exact location of where they were seated points toward an eyewitness memory.[9] Their question concerning her tears was a subtle rebuke, for there was no reason to be crying tears of sorrow when Jesus was alive. Her concern for Jesus's body is further evidence of her lack of understanding concerning his resurrection.

The exchange between Mary and Jesus is very moving. Thinking him to be the gardener, she hoped to learn where she could find Jesus's body. The moment he spoke her name she recognized his voice. Why did she not recognize him immediately?

---

[7] I do not comment on Mark 16:9–20 in my discussion of resurrection appearances due to the questions concerning its authenticity. For a brief discussion on this passage, see the *ESV Study Bible* (Wheaton, IL: Crossway, 2008); *The NIV Zondervan Study Bible* (Grand Rapids, MI: Zondervan, 2015); and the *Holman Christian Standard Study Bible* (Nashville: Holman Bible Publishers, 2015).

[8] John 20:11–18.

[9] "She saw two angels in white sitting where Jesus's body had been lying, one at the head and the other at the feet" (John 20:12).

Knowing for certain is difficult, and there may have been several factors involved. A combination of her tears, the darkness of the early morning hour, and the unpreparedness for him to be alive all may have played a part. We should remember that on numerous occasions after his resurrection his followers failed to recognize him immediately. Mary's embrace is the natural response of one who has an unexpected reunion with a loved one thought to be dead. Jesus communicated that she would see him again because he had not made his final ascent to the Father. Her mission was to report to the disciples that he was alive.

Jesus Appears to the Women Leaving the Tomb[10]

At some point after Jesus's encounter with Mary, and before the women's report to the disciples, Jesus met them. This appearance is the only one Matthew records in Jerusalem. Jesus confirmed to the women the reality of his resurrection and instructed them to tell the disciples he would meet them in Galilee. The women worshipped him and "took hold of his feet" (Matt 28:9), which reveals this was not a vision or some type of hallucination, but a physically resurrected Jesus: he was alive! In addition, the women's worship is an acknowledgment by both Jesus and the women of his deity, for worship is reserved only for God. The women obeyed Jesus's command to tell his disciples.

Jesus Appears to Peter[11]

At some point during the day, Jesus appeared privately to Simon Peter. Peter must have been in deep anguish after he looked into

---

[10] Matt 28:8–10.

[11] 1 Cor 15:5; Luke 24:34.

Jesus's eyes while in the high priest's courtyard. The examination of the empty tomb did little to diminish his brokenness. Nothing short of a face-to-face conversation with Jesus could restore this broken man. We are not told when, where, or what the conversation entailed, but Peter was a different man after he met the resurrected Savior.

Jesus Appears to Two Disciples Traveling to Emmaus[12]

Only Luke describes this event. This narrative is the longest in his Gospel. Later in the day on Sunday, Jesus walked with Cleopas and an unnamed companion from Jerusalem to Emmaus. Their eyes were providentially hindered from being able to recognize Jesus. The two men were overcome with sorrow, despite the women's report of an empty tomb and the appearance of angels. Along the way Jesus explained to them from Scripture the necessity of the Messiah's suffering and resurrection. When they arrived at Emmaus, two men implore Jesus to remain with them and eat the evening meal. As Jesus prayed, their eyes were opened to recognize him, and he disappeared. They returned immediately to Jerusalem to inform the disciples.

Jesus Appears to His Followers in the Upper Room (without Thomas present)[13]

As Cleopas and his friend were recounting their experience to the disciples who were gathered, Jesus suddenly appeared to them in the room despite the doors being locked. They must have experienced a myriad of emotions, ranging from utter shock to

---

[12] Luke 24:13–32.
[13] Luke 24:33–49; John 20:19–23.

unmitigated joy. The focus in Luke's account is on the physicality of Jesus's resurrection body. Jesus offered the disciples the opportunity to touch him. Unlike a spirit, he was able to eat what they had prepared. Luke makes perfectly clear the corporeal nature of Jesus's resurrection. Hallucinations and visions do not eat meals!

John describes Jesus commissioning his disciples and breathing on them, symbolically indicating that they would soon receive the Holy Spirit. While some believe the disciples received the Spirit in some manner at that time, I understand Jesus's breathing on them to foreshadow the disciples' reception of the Holy Spirit on the day of Pentecost. Jesus was abundantly clear that they were to preach a gospel that offered the forgiveness of sins. Thomas was conspicuously absent that evening. I wonder what Thomas must have thought when he returned only to learn that Jesus appeared to the group while he was gone.

Jesus Appears One Week Later to the Eleven (with Thomas present)[14]

A week later, Jesus appeared to the Eleven in the same location with Thomas present. Thomas has gone down in history with the nickname "Doubting Thomas," which is somewhat unfair. We should remember how the disciples doubted the testimony of the women. Later, when Jesus appeared to them, they were hiding behind locked doors. Thomas wanted physical proof— not just secondhand testimony—and that is exactly what he got! Thomas's response to Jesus's offer to touch his scars is one of the greatest expressions of faith in the Bible: "My Lord and my

---

[14] John 20:24–29.

God!" (John 20:28). Jesus commended the future faith of believers who do not have the opportunity see what Thomas saw.

These various appearances have raised questions concerning Jesus's resurrection body. He could suddenly appear in a room when the doors were locked. He could be in Emmaus in one moment and in the next moment have disappeared. He could be touched and even eat. Jesus's resurrection body had both continuity with his pre-resurrection body—he could eat and be touched; and discontinuity—he could be in one place at one moment and another place the next. Jesus's resurrection body is the prototype of the believer's future resurrection body. Paul taught extensively on the topic of the believer's resurrection body to the church at Corinth (1 Cor 15:35–49).

Jesus Appears to Seven Disciples at the Sea of Galilee[15]

We do not know how much time elapsed before Jesus's encounter with seven of his disciples at the Sea of Galilee. The narrative is straightforward, but its purpose may not be immediately clear. The meaning should not be found in allegorizing the number of fish caught (153) but rather in the act of fishing on the Sea of Galilee. When Jesus called his first four disciples, the setting was similar (Luke 5:1–11). Luke's account describes a miraculous catch of fish. The Sea of Galilee was where Jesus called these four fishermen to become fishers of people (v. 10). Just as they had a miraculous catch of fish that day, he called them to leave everything and follow him. He reminds them now of their original call.

---

[15] John 21:1–25.

Worldwide evangelization was on Jesus's heart as he taught his followers between his resurrection and ascension. On Resurrection Sunday, he breathed on the disciples and commissioned them to preach a gospel that offers forgiveness of sin. In both Luke and Matthew we find similar commissions to take the gospel to the world and to make disciples.[16] Since Jesus came to seek and save the lost, his followers must embrace the same purpose. Jesus does not want his church to be cloistered from the world. He wants his people to be in the world but not of the world (John 17:16).

After a delicious breakfast, Jesus turned his attention to Simon Peter (John 21:15–21). This passage records one of the most famous conversations in the Bible. If Peter was to lead, then he needed to be restored. Just as Peter denied Jesus three times in the presence of their enemy, now he must affirm his love for Jesus in the presence of his friends. Jesus calls Peter first to love and service and then to suffering and death. Peter would demonstrate his love for Jesus by shepherding Christ's sheep. In the upper room, Peter insisted he would die for Jesus; here Peter was told he would die a martyr's death.

Other Appearances to Followers in Galilee[17]

Jesus made numerous appearances to his followers over the forty days between his resurrection and ascension to heaven. Little is known about the location or the content of many of these encounters. At some point Jesus appeared to as many as five hundred followers in the Galilean hillside. In addition, Jesus

---

[16] Matt 28:19–20; Luke 24:44–48; John 20:19–22.

[17] Matt 28:16–20; 1 Cor 15:6–7.

appeared to his half-brother James. During Jesus's ministry his brothers did not believe in him (John 7:5). Later, James became one of the leading figures in the church in Jerusalem.

One of the most important post-resurrection appearances involved Jesus giving his followers the "Great Commission"—his marching orders for the church. Matthew 28:19–20 reads,

> Go, therefore, and make disciples of all nations, baptizing them in the name of the Father and of the Son and of the Holy Spirit, teaching them to observe everything I have commanded you. And remember, I am with you always, to the end of the age.

We do not know when this appearance took place, or which mountain is intended in verse 16. For this appearance to have taken place in Galilee would have been fitting, since it was where Jesus called them initially. As to why some doubted, we are not told. What is clear is the responsibility of the disciples to reproduce themselves by making disciples—going, baptizing, and teaching. The one who sent them has "all authority" (v. 18) and he would be with them wherever they went.

Jesus's Ascension[18]

Luke is the only author to describe Jesus's ascension, and he does so in both his Gospel and the book of Acts. The account in Acts is longer and clarifies the fact that Jesus ministered to his followers over a period of forty days after the resurrection. So, as Jesus's forty days came to an end, he returned to Judea, near Bethany. The disciples had already been instructed to remain in Jerusalem until the

---

[18] Luke 24:50–53; Acts 1:9–12.

coming of the Holy Spirit. Just as angels were present at Jesus's birth and resurrection, they were present at his return to heaven. The angels inform the disciples that just as Jesus ascended into heaven, he will return from heaven, bodily, visibly, and with the clouds. Now they must begin the work of world evangelization!

The Historicity of Jesus's Bodily Resurrection[19]

Jesus's bodily resurrection from the dead has been a source of debate from the beginning, and it remains a hot spot for the debate over the truthfulness of Christianity. As we have noted, the Roman guards and the Sanhedrin concocted a story that the disciples stole Jesus's body. Some still hold to this position. If the disciples stole the body, then they knew Jesus did not rise from the dead. What would they have gained? They certainly did not gain fame or fortune. Many of the disciples died a martyr's death and lived lives that were anything but opulent. People may die for a lie they believe to be true, but no one dies for a lie they know to be a lie. Furthermore, the Gospels describe the disciples hiding out in fear for their lives. This admission is so embarrassing, it is hard to believe the early church would have made up a story of the disciples' cowardice if it were not true. No, the disciples clearly could not have stolen Jesus's body.

Could the disciples have gone to the wrong tomb, which happened to be empty? Certainly, Joseph of Arimathea knew where his own tomb was located. Several women watched as Joseph and

---

[19] For extensive expansion of this discussion, see Licona, *The Resurrection of Jesus*; Wright, *The Resurrection of the Son of God*; Habermas and Licona, *The Case for the Resurrection of Jesus*; and Ladd, *I Believe in the Resurrection of Jesus*.

Nicodemus put Jesus's body in the tomb. The Roman soldiers knew where the tomb was located, and so must the Sanhedrin. If the disciples went to the wrong tomb, why did the Jewish leadership not present Jesus's corpse and silence the apostles' preaching in Jerusalem?

A once popular explanation, which is seldom argued today, is the swoon theory. This theory argues that Jesus only appeared to die on the cross but revived in the coolness of the damp tomb. Knowing what to say to such a ridiculous suggestion is difficult. Romans were experts at crucifixion. The agony and torment Jesus experienced before the cross caused many to die before crucifixion. Once an individual was impaled on a cross, death was certain. The men on either side of Jesus had their legs broken to precipitate their death, and Jesus's side was pierced to confirm his death. This theory provides no viable scenario where Jesus could escape physical death.

Another popular explanation is that Jesus's disciples were hallucinating when they thought they saw Jesus alive. The idea behind this theory is that as people grieve the death of a loved one, they are susceptible to hallucinating visions of them alive. Believing that so many people, in so many different settings, had similar kinds of hallucinations is impossible. On one occasion Jesus appeared to five hundred followers. Did all of those present have a hallucinating experience? Furthermore, why did the hallucinations end so abruptly for all these people? After forty days the original eyewitnesses did not report any more resurrection appearances. The hallucination theory just does not correspond to the historical evidence.

The historical evidence for Jesus's bodily resurrection from the dead is overwhelming. First, Jesus's followers demonstrated no premonition of a bodily resurrection. They were completely unprepared for it.

Second, the first witnesses of the resurrection were women. This is not the kind of story first-century Jewish men would fabricate. Women were often not considered very reliable witnesses; they were thought to be too emotional. The Gospels present the women as being much more levelheaded and courageous at Jesus's crucifixion and burial. If the disciples fabricated a story, it most certainly would involve Jesus appearing to them first.

Third, the transformation in Jesus's followers is unexplainable apart from the resurrection. The disciples in the book of Acts were bold and courageous. Peter preached with stunning courage to persons who just weeks before had condemned Jesus to death (Acts 4:1–22).

Fourth, the discovery of the empty tomb and the appearance of the angels are described succinctly and without great elaboration, much unlike the apocryphal accounts of Jesus's resurrection. If the stories were fabricated, one would expect much more elaborate descriptions.

Fifth, the early church began to gather for worship on Sunday, the first day of the week, instead of the Jewish Sabbath (Saturday). Something dramatic must have happened for the disciples to begin to gather for worship on the Lord's Day, the day of Jesus's resurrection.

Final Reflections

The implications of Jesus's bodily resurrection from the dead are numerous.[20]

---

[20] I am indebted to doctoral research student, Drew Smith, for the following points. Used with permission.

1. Jesus's resurrection establishes our eschatological hope.
For those who are united by faith to Jesus Christ, we have been
made new creations (2 Cor 5:17). Transformation, however, is a
gradual process. Little by little, the old self passes away, and the
new self is realized (Eph 4:20–24). At the end of this journey
stands Jesus Christ. He is the model, or paradigm, of who we aim to
become as Christians (2 Cor 3:18). More specifically, at the apex of
our metamorphosis stands the resurrected, incarnate Christ (Rom
6:4–11). Christians begin their journey through union with Jesus
in his death to sin. Likewise, we end that journey united with Jesus
in his resurrection from the dead. Furthermore, the truth of the
resurrection serves as a source of hope and inspiration for believers (1 Thess 4:17–18). When our earthly lives are complete, we
look toward the horizon—not to annihilation, nor judgment, nor
a diminished mode of existence—but fullness of life as completed
new creations in a world washed clean from sin (Rev 21:1–8).

2. Jesus's resurrection vindicates the Christian worldview.
Paul concluded his famous sermon to the Athenians with these
words: "Therefore, having overlooked the times of ignorance,
God now commands all people everywhere to repent, because he
has set a day when he is going to judge the world in righteousness by the man he has appointed. He has provided proof of this
to everyone by raising him from the dead" (Acts 17:30–31). The
heart of Paul's exhortation is a call for the Athenians to repent.
By this, Paul does not mean simply that they feel remorse for
their wrongdoing. Rather, the call to repentance is shorthand
for a summons to forsake idolatry and embrace the gospel of
Jesus Christ.[21] But what reason does Paul supply to motivate the

---

[21] John B. Polhill, *Acts*, The New American Commentary, vol. 26
(Nashville: B&H, 1992), 377.

Athenians to this course of action? The danger of a future judgment by "the man [God] has appointed" is, in context, a reference to Christ. Paul, however, did not stop his argument here. He proceeded to lend further support to the truth of the gospel and future judgment through an appeal to Jesus's resurrection. For Paul, the reality of the resurrection served as "proof" for the truth of Christianity from God (see Rom 1:4). Moreover, what held true in the Areopagus that day holds true here and now. The resurrection of Jesus Christ is the cornerstone upon which Christians support the truth of our worldview.

3. Jesus's resurrection was a conquest over the forces of darkness. Though unseen and often forgotten, the world we inhabit consists of both flesh and spirit. Behind the veil of our physical universe stands a vibrant world of spiritual beings. Within this world resides a demonic cohort, led by the devil, that seeks to wreak devastation on the earth—especially God's people (1 Pet 5:8). The author of Hebrews informs us that on the cross Jesus struck a blow against the devil: "Now since the children have flesh and blood in common, Jesus also shared in these, so that through his death he might destroy the one holding the power of death—that is, the devil" (Heb 2:14). Likewise, Paul expands this language of conquest over dark forces to include both Jesus's death and resurrection (Col 2:11–15). We may wonder, however, what it means for the devil to be "holding the power of death" and why this power serves as a source of fear for God's people. We should not conclude that Satan and God exist on a level footing.[22] Whatever authority and power Satan possesses, he gains only at the allowance of God himself (Job 1:9–12). God

---

[22] Thomas R. Schreiner, *Commentary on Hebrews*, Biblical Theology for Christian Proclamation series (Nashville: B&H, 2015), 104.

has granted Satan, for a season, the power of death with which to wreak his devastation on the world (Rev 20:1–3). Jesus, then, wins the victory over the devil, not by revoking his authority over death, nor by paying a ransom to him on our behalf. Instead, Jesus gains victory by rendering the devil's weapon of no effect. For those to whom the promise of the resurrection has been given, death holds no power (1 Cor 15:54–58). And where death proves powerless so, too, does the devil.

4. Jesus's resurrection motivates us for kingdom advancement. Before Jesus ascended into heaven, he left his followers with a mission of proclamation: making new disciples in every nation on the face of the earth (Matt 28:19–20). With this charge, however, came first a word of encouragement: "Jesus came near and said to them, 'All authority has been given to me in heaven and on earth'" (v. 18). A small cluster of disciples—bereft of wealth, power, or social status—were called by their Lord and Savior to scatter across the globe and proselytize the peoples of the earth. The mission was impossible, save for this one anchor of assurance: the One who possesses all authority went with them. The boldness of a believer to spread the gospel message does not come from confidence in his or her own station and abilities. Instead, our confidence flows from the knowledge that we serve the One who is seated on heaven's throne. And only through the resurrection do we gain knowledge of Jesus's cosmic standing.

Let us conclude our study with the famous greeting by early Christians: "The Lord has risen! He has risen, indeed!"

Hymn of Response

Christ the Lord is risen today, Alleluia!
Sons of men and angels say: Alleluia!

Raise your joys and triumphs high, Alleluia!
Sing, ye heav'ns, and earth, reply: Alleluia!

Lives again our glorious King, Alleluia!
Where, O death, is now thy sting? Alleluia!
Dying once He all doth save, Alleluia!
Where thy victory, O grave? Alleluia!

Love's redeeming work is done, Alleluia!
Fought the fight, the battle won, Alleluia!
Death in vain forbids him rise, Alleluia!
Christ hath opened Paradise, Alleluia!

Lives again our glorious King, Alleluia!
Where, O death, is now thy sting? Alleluia!
Once he died our souls to save, Alleluia!
Where's thy victory, boasting grave? Alleluia!

Soar we now where Christ has led, Alleluia!
Following our exalted Head, Alleluia!
Made like Him, like Him we rise, Alleluia!
Ours the cross, the grave, the skies, Alleluia![23]

---

[23] Charles Wesley, "Christ the Lord Is Risen Today," 1739, *Baptist Hymnal*, #270.

GROUP STUDY GUIDE

As you read through *Jesus's Final Week: From Triumphal Entry to Empty Tomb*, I hope you are

- enlivened by the truths of Passion Week
- encouraged to engage the study with a genuine heart-hunger for personal and group Bible study
- compelled to gather in corporate worship in praise for the risen Christ
- drawn together in true friendship and community with other believers
- impassioned to tell unbelievers the great truths to be discovered as we walk together with Jesus through Passion Week

Each week you will read through one or two chapters and then meet with your group to discuss what you have learned about the most important week in human history. May God bless your study and fellowship!

Each week:

- Pray for your group leader and the group members by name.

- If your group is doing this study leading up to Passion Week and Easter Sunday, pray for your minister(s) as they prepare your congregation for Easter worship services.
- Pray for visitors who will be in attendance on Easter Sunday. Invite a friend, neighbor, or coworker to attend with you.

Week 1

Read the introduction and chapters 1 and 2 in preparation for the group study.

Discussion:

1. Have someone read John 12:1–8 for the group. We see Mary's extravagant devotion in anointing Jesus with the expensive perfume. She humbled herself further and honored Jesus by letting down her hair to cleanse his feet and rub the costly perfume into his skin.
    a. Group discussion: Has there been a time in your spiritual life when Christ's call to "come, follow me" has been personally costly for you?
    b. Were there things or relationships that you had to give up? In what ways were your actions personally humbling for you?
    c. Personal reflection: Are there things that are currently keeping you from honoring and worshipping Jesus as you should? Are you willing to give up these costly things?
2. John 12:3 describes an eyewitness memory of when the aroma of the perfume filled the room. Sharing memories

from our walk with Christ strengthens bonds with other believers.

    a. Group discussion: Is there a specifically vivid memory from your conversion or recent walk with Jesus that you would like to share with the group?

    b. Why do we need to share our spiritual memories with others?

3. Have someone read Luke 19:37–44. With his entry into Jerusalem, Jesus openly proclaimed his messiahship. He wept and mourned over Jerusalem because most of the people failed to understand that he was the Messiah.

    a. Group discussion: Why do many believers fail to mourn for the lost? How can we develop a greater concern for persons who do not know Jesus? Who do you need to talk to about Jesus?

    b. Ask the group to share the first names of those they know who need to come to faith in Jesus. Have group members write down the names, and ask them to pray for these individuals during the coming weeks.

4. Have someone read Matt 21:18–22. Like the fig tree, Jesus desires his people to bear spiritual fruit for his glory.

    a. Group discussion: What spiritual fruit is Jesus looking for in our lives?

    b. Personal reflection: What cultivation and pruning needs to take place in your life to produce that fruit?

5. Have someone read Mark 11:15–18. As discussed in chapter 2, the temple was a sacred place designed for worship of a holy God by his chosen people. The religious leaders' callous disregard for true worship led to the destruction of the physical temple in AD 70. However, Jesus's holy, sacrificial death on the cross and

resurrection established a new covenant, and thereby a new temple has been established as the Holy Spirit now lives in each believer (1 Cor 3:16–17).

    a.   Group discussion: What ways can believers compromise their worship of a holy God?

    b.   Read 1 Pet 1:13–16. How can Christians work out this call to holiness in an unholy world?

6. Ask the group to read chapters 3 and 4 before next week's session.

7. Close in prayer. Have group members pray for each other.

8. Pray for those considered earlier who need to come to faith in Jesus.

9. Ask group members to pray for wisdom about individuals they may invite to attend Easter service with them.

Week 2

Read chapters 3 and 4 in preparation for the group study.

Introduction:

In the passages we study this week, Jesus battled with his enemies. The religious leaders asked Jesus questions designed to discredit him with his followers and provide them with the grounds to destroy him. However, these questions were a spiritual battlefield for which Jesus was well prepared.

Discussion:

1. Have someone read Matt 21:12–13, 23–27 for the group. When Jesus entered the temple on Tuesday morning, he

was approached by a group of temple leaders demanding to know under whose authority he was acting when he cleared the temple. Their question goes beyond the temple clearing and really asked where he claimed the authority for his teaching and ministry to have come from.

a. Group discussion: Instead of providing a direct answer to their leading question, Jesus asked them where John's baptism came from (whose authority— heaven or human). Why did Jesus respond this way?

b. Jesus went on to tell three parables (Matt 21:28– 22:14) in condemnation of the religious leaders' hypocrisy.

   i. What was Jesus's main point in the parable of the Two Sons? How is it possible for a believer to act more like the second son than the first?

   ii. What is the main point in Jesus's second parable? How can the church be the kind of vinegrowers that are pleasing to God (Matt 21:43)?

   iii. What was Jesus's main point in the third parable? Why are those from the "highways and byways" more responsive to the invitation than those originally invited? What does it mean for the guest not to be dressed in "wedding clothes"? What happened to this guest?

   iv. Personal reflection: What evidence could one offer that they are dressed in the proper attire?

2. Have someone read Mark 12:28–34. Pharisees, Herodians, and Sadducees had come forward with questions designed to attack and discredit Jesus; and all had failed

as Jesus explained God's authority over money, earthly leaders, and even death.

a. A scribe posed a question about the greatest commandment. In the ensuing conversation Jesus commented to the scribe, "You are not far from the kingdom of God." What did Jesus mean by this comment? What do you think Jesus saw in this scribe and his question that was different from all the other questioners?

b. In Jesus's response to the scribe's question on the greatest commandment, he answered that we must love God! But he also provided the second greatest and corresponding commandment that we must love others as ourselves. Why did Jesus connect these two commands together?

    i. Ask group members to share how someone in the group or your church has shown God's love to them (ministered to them) recently.

    ii. Personal action: What specific action can you take this week to show God's love to someone?

3. Have someone read Mark 12:38–44. Describe the scribes' and the widow's actions.

a. Group discussion: Why did Jesus point out the widow's actions to his disciples? Was this widow's gift only about money?

b. Personal reflection: Is there something specific I can do this week to reflect the attitude of the widow?

4. As Jesus left Jerusalem on that Tuesday, he taught his disciples both about the coming judgment and destruction of Jerusalem (in AD 70) and about his own second

coming. One major element of his teaching is the need for his disciples to be prepared to be persecuted for proclaiming the gospel and faithful service. Jesus also warned his followers to be watchful as we wait for his return.

   a. Group discussion: In Matt 25:1–30 Jesus told the parables of the Ten Virgins and the Talents.

      i.   How do these parables emphasize the need for faithful service?

      ii. How do these parables emphasize the need for watchfulness?

      iii. What excuses do people offer to avoid serving Christ in the church as they await his coming?

   b. Personal reflection: Ask someone in the group to pray that group members would exhibit faithful service to Jesus as they await his coming.

5. On Tuesday of Passion Week Jesus spoke with stinging criticism of the religious leaders. We can see that the scribes and Pharisees were often focused on doing the right things but for the wrong reasons.

   a. What was lacking in the religious leaders?

   b. How can we tell when we are doing the right things for the wrong reasons?

6. Ask the group to read chapter 5 before next week's session.

7. Close in prayer. Have group members pray for each other.

8. Pray for those who need to come to faith in Jesus.

9. Ask group members to pray for wisdom about individuals they may invite to attend Easter service with them.

Week 3

Read chapter 5 in preparation for the group study.

Introduction:

In chapter 5 we see Jesus celebrating the Passover meal with his disciples and instituting the Lord's Supper. We will look at several key elements of this Thursday evening as we walk with Jesus through Passion Week.

Discussion:

1. Have someone read John 13:1–15 for the group. As Jesus and his disciples gathered to celebrate the Passover, Jesus took on the role of a humble servant and washed the disciples' feet. But this simple act was not just an act of kindness and cleanliness, which a host would normally have a servant perform. Washing the disciples' feet was a symbolic act with theological significance.
    a. Group discussion: In John 13:8, Jesus replied to Peter, "If I don't wash you, you have no part with me." What did Jesus mean by this statement?
    b. Peter loved Jesus and requested that not only his feet be washed but also his hands and head. What is the significance of Jesus's response in verse 10?
    c. Personal reflection: Do you need to be cleansed from a specific sin you are battling presently?
2. Take five to ten minutes to discuss the similarities and differences between the Passover meal and the Last Supper as mentioned in "The Last Supper" section of chapter 5 of the book.

    a. How did the shedding of Jesus's blood establish a new covenant?

    b. Why is personal faith necessary to fully understand, participate in, and celebrate the Lord's Supper?

    c. How can you prepare yourself better to partake of the Lord's Supper to make it more meaningful and beneficial to you?

3. Have someone read Luke 22:24–30. On Thursday evening Jesus washed the disciples' feet, led them through the Passover meal, instituted the Lord's Supper, and predicted his betrayal and death.

    a. Next, we read about the disciples' arguments over who was the greatest among them (the third time they have held this argument). Why did the disciples (and us!) find it so difficult to embrace Jesus's approach to greatness?

    b. Personal reflection: How can you practice Jesus's model of servant leadership in your life this next week? Share with the group.

4. Read Luke 22:31–34. Jesus spoke to Simon Peter as the leader of the disciples. Jesus predicted that Satan would "sift" them ("you" is plural, referring to the entire group).

    a. How would Peter and the disciples be "sifted" in the coming hours?

    b. Personal Reflection: Jesus is seated at God's right hand praying for his people. How does the knowledge that Jesus is praying for you change your perspective on your trials and difficulties?

5. Jesus was leaving them, although he promised them the Holy Spirit, and he provided extensive teaching about

the Spirit. In your own words, state the teaching about the Holy Spirit found in each passage.

   a.   John 14:15–17, 27

   b.   John 15:26–27

   c.   John 16:7–15

6. Ask the group to read chapters 6 and 7 before next week's session.

7. Close in prayer. Have group members pray for each other.

8. Pray for those who need to come to faith in Jesus.

9. Ask group members to pray for wisdom about individuals they may invite to attend Easter service with them.

Week 4

Read chapters 6 and 7 in preparation for the group study.

Chapter 6—The Garden of Gethsemane

Introduction:

We begin this week's walk with Jesus in the garden of Gethsemane. He told his inner circle (Peter, James, and John) that he was "grieved to the point of death" (Mark 14:34). Luke 22:44 tells us that "his sweat became like drops of blood falling to the ground." Indeed, the weight of the world's sins was pressing down upon him!

Discussion:

1. Jesus had predicted his death and crucifixion several times before crowds and his closest disciples. We have seen his suffering and death as the fulfillment of many Scripture passages and that he was both aware of his

coming death and sovereignly in charge of all the events leading up to this point.

    a. Group discussion: In Luke 22:42 Jesus says, "Father, if you are willing, take this cup away from me." This verse communicates the very real struggle Jesus was experiencing. However, Jesus follows this by saying to the Father, "Not my will, but yours, be done." What was Jesus saying when he asked God, "Take this cup away from me"?

    b. What should we understand from "Not my will, but yours, be done"?

    c. Are you praying about a specific matter and need to complete the prayer with "Not my will, but yours, be done"? Can you share it with the group?

2. We cannot know the depth of the agony Jesus experienced as he knowingly faced his future of betrayal, abandonment, beatings, mocking, crucifixion, and death. Amid this incredible emotional and physical pain, he also had to bear the sins of the entire world and the abandonment of God. No wonder his prayer was anguished!

    a. In the end, Jesus's time in prayer strengthened his resolve to follow God's plan. Ask group members to share a time when they experienced anguish in prayer and how God answered.

    b. Does God always answer our prayers in the affirmative? Why? Has there been a time God answered one of your prayers as no, and looking back, you see God's grace in it?

    c. Personal reflection: Knowing God strengthens us when we pray, why is prayer such a struggle for many Christians to engage in consistently?

3. The arresting mob appeared, and the kiss of betrayal was bestowed on Jesus. In the chaos of that night a sword was swung and an ear was severed. The situation could have easily careened out of control, but Jesus maintained control and directed the actions of his followers, his enemies, and the Roman soldiers.

   a. Have someone read John 18:3–12 for the group. How did Jesus demonstrate himself to be the Good Shepherd in those tense moments?

   b. Can you share a recent experience when Jesus the Good Shepherd protected you? How can we become more aware of Jesus's daily care for us as the Good Shepherd?

Chapter 7—The Jewish Trials

Introduction:

Jesus was dragged from the garden into the presence of his chief opponents, the religious leadership. Jesus, the sinless Son of God, was on trial for his life. He endured false testimony and accusations; and an unjust judge declared the righteous Son of God to be guilty of blasphemy and sentenced him to death.

Discussion:

4. Have someone read 1 Pet 2:21–25. How does this passage inform our understanding of Jesus's trial before the Sanhedrin? Why is it so difficult for us to follow Jesus's example?

5. Have someone read Luke 22:54–62 and Matt 27:3–10.

   a. How are Peter and Judas's actions similar?

   b. How are Peter and Judas's actions different?

    c. Why did Peter and Judas respond so differently when they realized the consequences of their actions?

6. Dr. Cook makes the following statement in chapter 7: "Judas is a painful reminder of how close a person can be to Jesus but not experience saving grace." What evidence would indicate this may be true of a person?

7. Ask the group to read chapters 8 and 9 before next week's session.

8. Close in prayer. Have group members pray for each other.

9. Pray for those who need to come to faith in Jesus.

10. Ask group members to pray for wisdom about individuals they may invite to attend Easter service with them.

Week 5

Read chapters 8 and 9 in preparation for the group study.

Chapter 8—The Roman Trial: Guilty of Treason

Introduction:

The religious leaders pronounced Jesus to be guilty of blasphemy and worthy of death. However, being ruled by the Romans they were powerless to act and therefore delivered Jesus to Pontius Pilate for trial.

Discussion:

1. Have someone read Matt 27:11–26 to the group. Pilate rightly ignored the false charges and was interested only in the charge that Jesus was King of the Jews. He understood quickly that Jesus had done nothing worthy of

death. However, the religious leaders (and the crowds) were insistent upon crucifixion. Pilate, wishing to disassociate himself from the bloodguilt of Jesus's death, washed his hands publicly, saying "See to it yourselves" (v. 24).

    a. How did Jesus's and Pilate's understanding of kingdom differ?

    b. In what ways did Pilate seek to avoid having to render a verdict on Jesus?

    c. In what ways does the release of Barabbas symbolize a believer's release from judgment?

    d. The crowds yelled, "His blood be on us and on our children!" (v. 25). How do children suffer for the sins of their parents?

2. Read John 19:12–16. Fear, authority, and guilt continue to be the key issues in this passage.

    a. Discuss the chief priests' response to Pilate, "We have no king but Caesar!" (v. 15). This statement is astounding in so many ways. The Jews hated the Romans. They hated the taxes the Romans imposed. They hated the Roman presence in the holy city and the authority the Roman's exercised. How do Christians sometimes choose government over God?

Chapter 9—The Crucifixion and Death of Jesus Christ

Introduction:

Pilate, having submitted to the demands of the religious leaders and the crowds, had Jesus flogged and delivered to be crucified. Let us look at some of the events of the crucifixion and Jesus's words from the cross.

Discussion:

3. Have someone read Luke 6:28 and 23:34. Jesus continued to focus on others, even on the cross. How amazing!
   a. How was Jesus faithful to his own teaching?
   b. Can you think of someone in your life that you need to forgive for their past sin against you? How can forgiveness bring about freedom? How is bitterness a form of bondage?

4. Have someone read John 19:19–22. Pilate was intentional with his insult, making sure it was written in all three languages commonly spoken by those who attended the Passover festival.
   a. How was what Pilate wrote about Jesus ironic?
   b. What other ironies do you see in the crucifixion narrative?

5. Read Luke 23:39–43. From the other Gospels we learn that at least for a time, both criminals crucified with Jesus mocked him. But an amazing change of heart happened with one of the criminals.
   a. How can we explain this criminal's change of heart?
   b. What elements of this criminal's words show his repentance?
   c. What spiritual lesson(s) can we learn from the repentant thief?

6. Read Jesus's words in Mark 15:34.
   a. How can we understand Jesus's words as a cry of desolation and abandonment?
   b. How can we understand Jesus's words as an expression of faith, trust, and victory?

7. Read John 19:30.
   a. What did Jesus mean when he said, "It is finished"? See John 4:34 and 17:4.
   b. Why do you think Jesus never lost sight of his purpose in coming?

8. Read Mark 15:38. Discuss the significance of the tearing of the temple curtain from top to bottom. What practical importance does this event have in your life?

9. Read Mark 15:39. This centurion probably directed and likely participated in the brutality of crucifying Jesus. Yet, as Jesus breathed his last breath, this hardened Roman soldier declared, "Truly this man was the Son of God!" What events did the centurion witness that contributed to his confession?

10. On this Friday of Passion Week, our walk with Jesus concludes with his death on the cross. His death was confirmed by Pilate, and his body was released to Joseph of Arimathea and Nicodemus for burial (John 19:38–42). Why is the appearance of Nicodemus surprising? Nicodemus is mentioned in three passages within John's Gospel (chapters 3, 7, and 19). Read them as a group and discuss what each teaches about him.

11. Ask the group to read chapter 10 before next week's session.

12. Close in prayer. Have group members pray for each other.

13. Pray for those who need to come to faith in Jesus.

14. Ask group members to pray for and invite someone to attend Easter service with them.

Week 6

Read chapter 10 in preparation for the group study.

Introduction:

Last week we walked the road to Golgotha with Jesus. We witnessed his brutal crucifixion and death. But the story has not ended. This week we walk with Jesus through his glorious resurrection. A series of rapidly unfolding events occurred as recorded by the four Gospel writers.

Discussion:

1. Throughout the Gospels, the disciples are presented regularly as being slow to understand Jesus's teaching. Jesus told them repeatedly that he would suffer and die by crucifixion but that he would rise from the dead after three days. These same disciples were now hidden away in fear with apparently no memory of Jesus's words and certainly no expectation that he was going to rise from the dead.

   a. What events indicate that Jesus's followers were not expecting him to rise from the dead?

   b. Discuss the various reactions of Jesus's followers, including their range of emotions (Mary Magdalene, the other women, Peter, John, and the rest of the disciples).

2. Have someone read Luke 24:13–49.

   a. In verses 19–21, how did the two men characterize Jesus's words and deeds?

   b. Personal reflection: In verses 25–27 Jesus mildly rebukes the unbelief of the two and then explains from Moses, the Prophets, and all the Scriptures the necessity for the Messiah to suffer and then be glorified. Talk about in-depth Bible study! No wonder their hearts burned inside them as Jesus spoke. Why do you think so many believers do not experience a great hunger for the Word from reading the Bible? What changes need to take place regarding your commitment to the Word? Have a group member pray for the group to have a deeper hunger for God's Word.

c. In verse 31, what is the significance of the phrase "their eyes were opened"?

d. The two rushed back to Jerusalem to tell the Eleven that they had seen the risen Christ, and Jesus appeared in their midst. Why did Jesus ask for something to eat? How was Jesus's pre-resurrection body and post-resurrection body similar, yet different? Have someone read 1 Cor 15:35–58. What do you learn from this passage about the believer's future resurrection body? What impact should this have on the way we live today?

3. Have someone read John 21:15–19. Peter's three denials must have still weighed heavily on him. After breakfast, with the six others mentioned in verse 2, Jesus restored Peter.

a. How many times did Jesus question Peter about his love? What is the significance? What did Jesus call Peter to do in the present and in the future?

b. Jesus mentioned a common theme during many of his appearances—Get to work! Jesus came to seek and save the lost, and through his resurrection appearances he commissioned his disciples (and all his followers) to do the same. Have the group discuss Jesus's Great Commission in Matt 28:18–20. What did Jesus command them to do?

    c. Have each person in the group discuss their Great Commission "mission field."

4. Close in prayer. Have group members pray for each other.

5. Pray for those who need to come to faith in Jesus.

6. Pray for your pastor as he prepares the Easter sermon.

7. Ask group members to pray for and invite someone to attend Easter service with them.

8. Conclude the session with the group saying, "The Lord is risen! He is risen, indeed!"

NAME AND SUBJECT INDEX

A

abomination of desolation, 44–46
Alexander (son of Simon of
    Cyrene), 121
angel of death, 65
angels, 34, 145–46, 148, 155
Annas, 94, 96–97
Antichrist, 45
Antiochus Epiphanes, 45

B

Barabbas, 113–15, 124
Bethany, 1–3, 11, 23, 42, 48, 53
Bethphage, 6
blasphemy charge, 95–96, 99, 109

C

Caesar, 33, 112, 115–16. *See also*
    Tiberius
Caiaphas, 94, 96–97, 106
centurion's confession, 136
chief priests, the, 11, 53–54, 102,
    110–11, 113–15, 129–30, 137
Church of the Holy Sepulchre,
    122
church, the, xiii, 30, 35–36, 50, 78,
    89, 153–54, 157
Cleopas, 150

cross, 83, 123, 139
crucifixion, 123, 156
cup of God's wrath, 83–84
cursing of the fig tree, 16–18, 23,
    27–28

D

David, 9, 30, 36, 64, 87
denarius (denarii), 4, 32, 39
devil, 61, 159–60
disciples, 5–6, 11, 23, 40, 42, 61,
    63, 71, 74–77, 85, 89, 139,
    150–54

E

earthquake, 46, 136, 145
Emmaus, 144, 148, 150
evangelism, 153, 155

F

faith, 23, 31, 47, 71, 77, 131, 133,
    152
Farewell Discourse, 74–77
Feast of Unleavened Bread, 60
foot washing, 62
forgiveness, 23, 67, 70, 102, 128–
    29, 151

fulfillment of Scripture, 7–9, 12, 64–65, 72–73, 88, 103, 135, 138, 150

G

Galilee, 12, 111–12, 144, 146, 149, 154
garden of Gethsemane, 76, 81–89
Golgotha, 122
gospel, 151, 153, 159–60
Gospels, xiii, xv, 1, 63
Great Commission, 144, 153–54

H

Hallel psalms, 9, 67
Herod Antipas, 111–13
Herodians, the, 32
Herodias, 112
Herod the Great, 18–19, 110, 112
Holy Spirit, 36, 43, 71, 75–76, 140, 151, 155
Holy Week, xiii, xv
hope (in Jesus), 47, 158

I

Israel, xiii, 8–9, 12, 17–18, 30, 37, 65–66

J

James (brother of Jesus), 154
James (disciple), 82
Jerusalem, xiii, 1–2, 7–8, 10, 12, 18, 38, 110, 121, 144, 148, 154
    destruction of, 10, 39–41, 43–46, 116
Jesus
    agony, 82–85, 156
    anointing, 3–6, 144–45
    arrest, 19, 30, 53, 89–90
    ascension, 144, 154–55
    authority of, 28, 154
    betrayal, 85–88, 104
    burial, 5, 138–39
    condemnation, 96, 100, 114, 115–16
    crucifixion, 113–14, 119–35
    death, 72–73, 123–24, 132, 135–38
    historicity of resurrection, 155–57
    mocking, 99, 112, 120, 130–31, 139
    resurrection, 143–54
    second coming, 40–41, 46–48, 50, 106
    suffering, 68, 88, 116, 125, 140, 150
    trial, 94–100, 109–17
Joanna, 130
John (disciple), 60, 82, 130, 146–47
John the Baptist, 28–29, 112
Joseph of Arimathea, 138–39, 145, 155
Judah (son of Jacob), 8–9
Judas, 4–5, 53, 61, 86, 137
    betrayal, 6, 54–55, 63–65, 86, 104–5
    death, 101–4
Judea, 154
judgment, 17, 30, 38, 43, 132

K

Kidron Valley, 18, 42, 81
kingdom of God, 9, 29, 31, 68, 125, 131
kingship, 8, 11, 20, 111, 113, 131

L

Last Supper, 61–71, 115
Law, 33, 35, 97

Lazarus, 3
Lord's Supper, 77–78
    consubstantiation, 68
    memorial, 70
    transubstantiation, 68
love, 35, 61, 75, 145, 153

M

Malchus, 88
Mary Magdalene, 129–30, 146,
    148–49
Mary, mother of Jesus, 129–30
Mary of Bethany, 2–6, 54
Mary, wife of Clopas, 129–30
Maundy Thursday, 59
Messiah, 1, 8–9, 36, 38, 43, 100,
    106, 115, 137, 150
    Messianic Age, 22
    messianic identity, 1, 11
Mishnah, 95, 99
Mount of Olives, 9, 12, 42, 106

N

new covenant, 67, 70–71, 77
Nicodemus, 138, 145, 156

O

obedience, 62, 67, 75
Olivet Discourse, 39–48

P

Palm Sunday, xiii, 1
parables, 29–31, 41, 46, 48
Passion Narrative, 73. See also
    Jesus: death
Passion Week. See Holy Week
Passover, 2, 9, 60, 65–71, 88, 95,
    113, 137
Pentecost, 151
persecution, 43, 76

Peter, 11, 60, 62, 73–74, 82, 88,
    116, 140, 146–47, 149–50,
    153, 157
    denial, 94, 100–101, 104–6
Pharisees, the, 11, 32, 37–38, 49,
    106, 115
poll-tax, 32–33
Pontius Pilate, 109–15, 117, 119–
    20, 129, 137, 145
praetorium, 110–11, 120
prayer, 23, 73, 76, 81–85, 90, 129,
    139
prophetic acts, 1, 15

R

religious leaders, 11, 19, 23, 29–31,
    53, 96, 106, 114, 116, 145
repentance, 29, 102, 105, 158
resurrection, 33–34, 136–37
    resurrection body, 152
    Resurrection Sunday, xvi, 148,
        153
Roman rule, 20, 32, 54, 110, 116,
    121
Roman soldiers, 86, 119–20,
    145–46, 155
Rufus (son of Simon of Cyrene),
    121

S

Sadducees, the, 33–34, 95
Salome, 129–30
salvation, 116, 131
Sanhedrin, 28, 94–100, 102, 106,
    109, 114, 138, 146, 155
Satan, 5, 54, 61, 65, 73–74, 85,
    101, 105, 159–60
scribes, the, 11, 37–38, 49, 106,
    130
Sea of Galilee, 152–53
servant leadership, 71–72

seven sayings of Jesus, 125–29,
      139–40
Shema, the, 35
Simeon, 130
Simon of Cyrene, 121
Simon the leper, 3
sin, 49, 54, 62, 67, 70, 78, 83, 105,
      116, 125, 129, 134–35, 140,
      151, 153, 158
Song of the Vineyard, 29
Son of God, 49, 98–100, 136
sovereignty of God, 43, 55, 64, 77,
      90, 103
Stephen, 125–26, 140

T

temple, 12, 19, 28, 38–39, 42, 55,
      97–98
      clearing of, 16, 18–22

Court of the Gentiles, 20–21
curtain, 135
destruction of, 16–17, 44–45,
      116, 136
Temple Mount, 9
Ten Commandments, 35
Thomas, 151–52
Tiberius (Caesar), 32–33, 112
Titus, 45
tomb, 145–47, 155
Torah, 34
triumphal entry, 1–2, 6–10, 30
Tyropoeon Valley, 18

W

widow's offering, 38–39, 49
women, 122, 129, 138, 144–46,
      149, 155, 157
wrath of God, 135

SCRIPTURE INDEX

Genesis
2:8–9 *132*
24:11 *60*
37:28 *55*
44:18–34 *9*
49:10 *9*
49:10–11 *8*

Exodus
3:6 *34*
3:15–16 *34*
6:6 *68*
6:6–7 *65–66*
10:22 *132–33*
12:13 *66*
12:23 *66*
12:46 *138*
20:2–11 *35*
20:12 *126*
20:12–17 *35*
21:32 *55*
24:8 *70*
28 *124*
30:11–16 *21*
39:27–29 *124*

Leviticus
16:4 *124*
19:18 *35*

Numbers
14:6 *99*
19:2 *7*
35:30 *97*

Deuteronomy
6:4–5 *35*
17:6 *97*
19:15 *97*
21:3 *7*
21:6–8 *114*
21:22–24 *123–24*
25:5–10 *33*

1 Samuel
6:7 *7*
15:22 *49*

2 Samuel
7:12–13 *36*
15:5 *87*
20:8–10 *87*

1 Kings
1:32–48 *9*
8:41–43 *22*
18:13 *30*
19:10 *30*
19:14 *30*

2 Kings
23:1–7 *20*

2 Chronicles
29:3–11 *20*

Nehemiah
9:26 *30*

Job
1:9–12 *159*
19:26 *34*

Psalms
8:2 *11*
16:9–11 *34*
22 *133*
22:1 *127, 133*
22:1–21 *133*
22:7 *130*
22:15 *127, 135*
22:18 *124–25*
22:22–31 *133*
26:6 *114*
31:5 *128*
41:9 *64*
49:15 *34*
69:21 *122–23, 127, 135*

73:13 *114*
73:25–26 *34*
102:26 *47*
110 *36*
110:1 *36, 98*
113–14 *67*
113–18 *9*
115–18 *68*
118 *30*
118:22–23 *30*
118:25–26 *9*

Proverbs

1:24–26 *116–17*
14:31 *6*
19:17 *6*
22:9 *6*
27:6 *87*

Isaiah

5:1–7 *29*
10:5 *65*
11:1 *37*
11:11–16 *66*
26:19 *34*
29:3 *10*
34:4 *17*
35:1–10 *66*
40:1–5 *66*
51:6 *47*
51:17 *84*
52:13–53:12 *65*
53:4–5 *73*
53:6 *134*
53:7 *98*
53:10 *134*
53:12 *124, 128*
55:8–9 *90*
56:7 *21–22*
59:1–2 *133*
62:11 *7*

Jeremiah

6:6–21 *10*
7:11 *22*
7:16–20 *21*
8:13 *17*
19 *103*
19:1–13 *103*
23:1 *65*
23:5–6 *37*
23:5–8 *66*
23:15 *83–84*
25:15 *84*
26:20–23 *30*
31:31–34 *70*
52:4–5 *10*

Lamentations

2:15 *130*

Ezekiel

1:28 *87*
4:1–3 *10*
37:1–14 *34*
44:4 *87*

Daniel

2:46 *87*
7:13 *98*
7:13–14 *46*
8:18 *87*
9:27 *44*
10:9 *87*
11:31 *44*
12:2 *34*
12:11 *44*

Hosea

2:14–15 *66*
9:10 *17–18*

Amos

3:7 *30*
8:9–10 *132*

Habakkuk

1:13 *134*
2:11 *11*

Zechariah

1:6 *30*
9:9 *7–8, 12*
11 *103*
11:12–13 *55, 103*
12:10 *73, 138*
13:7 *72, 88*
13:7–9 *72*
14:4 *9*

Matthew

5:43–44 *35*
10:17–25 *76*
13:45–46 *39*
14:23 *54*
19:19 *35*
20:6 *120*
21–28 *xiii*
21:1–7 *6*
21:1–9 *1*
21:4–7 *7*
21:8–9 *9*
21:10–11 *10*
21:12–13 *18, 166*
21:14–17 *10*
21:15 *11*
21:16 *11*
21:18–21 *23*
21:18–22 *16, 165*
21:19 *16*
21:21 *23*
21:23–27 *166*
21:23–22:14 *28*

21:23–23:39 *28*
21:28–32 *29*
21:28–22:14 *167*
21:31 *29*
21:33–46 *29*
21:43 *31, 167*
22:1–14 *31*
22:13 *31*
22:15–22 *32*
22:23–33 *33*
22:30 *34*
22:34–40 *34*
22:41–46 *36*
23:1–39 *37*
23:37 *10*
23:37–39 *37–38*
23:39 *38*
24:1–3 *41–42*
24:1–35 *40*
24:1–25:46 *39*
24:3 *42*
24:4–14 *41–42*
24:9–14 *76*
24:13–28 *41*
24:15 *54*
24:15–20 *45*
24:15–28 *44*
24:21–28 *45*
24:29–31 *41, 46*
24:32–41 *46*
24:36–51 *40*
24:42–44 *41*
24:42–25:30 *48*
24:45–51 *41*
25:1–30 *169*
25:14–30 *41*
25:31–46 *35, 41*
26:6 *3*
26:6–13 *2*
26:14–15 *5*
26:14–16 *54*
26:15–16 *105*
26:17–19 *60*

26:17–35 *59*
26:20 *61*
26:21–25 *63*
26:26–29 *69*
26:36–46 *81*
26:39 *91*
26:47–56 *85*
26:57–68 *94, 97*
26:62–63 *98*
26:64 *98*
26:65 *99*
26:69–75 *100*
27:1 *100*
27:2 *110*
27:3–5 *101*
27:3–10 *55, 101, 103, 174*
27:4 *102*
27:5 *102*
27:6 *102*
27:8 *102*
27:11 *111*
27:11–14 *110*
27:11–26 *175*
27:15–26 *113*
27:16 *114*
27:19 *114*
27:20–22 *114*
27:24 *114, 176*
27:25 *114, 176*
27:27–31 *120*
27:31–34 *121*
27:31–66 *119*
27:34 *122*
27:35 *124*
27:35–44 *122*
27:38 *124*
27:39–40 *130*
27:42 *130*
27:44 *131*
27:45 *132*
27:45–50 *132*

27:46 *83, 127, 133*
27:51 *136*
27:51–52 *136*
27:51–56 *135*
27:54 *136*
27:55–56 *130*
27:57–58 *137*
27:59–66 *138*
27:62–66 *139*
28:1–2 *145*
28:1–8 *145*
28:1–20 *143*
28:2–8 *146*
28:3 *145*
28:4 *145*
28:6 *146*
28:8–10 *149*
28:9 *149*
28:11–15 *139, 145–46*
28:16 *154*
28:16–20 *153*
28:18 *154, 160*
28:18–20 *181*
28:19–20 *153–54, 160*

Mark

1:2 *103*
2:9 *99*
3:6 *53*
4:17 *73*
8:29 *11, 101*
8:33–37 *71*
9:2–9 *101*
9:35 *35*
10:35–45 *71*
10:43–44 *35*
11–16 *xiii*
11:1 *3*
11:1–7 *6*
11:1–10 *1*

11:8–10 *9*
11:9 *9*
11:11 *3*
11:12 *3*
11:12–14 *16*
11:13 *16*
11:14 *16*
11:15–17 *16*
11:15–18 *165*
11:15–19 *18*
11:16 *21*
11:17 *21–22*
11:18 *19*
11:19 *23*
11:20 *23*
11:20–25 *16, 23*
11:21 *16*
11:23–24 *23*
11:25 *23*
11:27–12:12 *28*
11:27–12:40 *28*
12:1–12 *29*
12:9 *30*
12:10–11 *30*
12:13–17 *32*
12:17 *33*
12:18–27 *33*
12:28 *35*
12:28–34 *34, 167*
12:34 *36*
12:35 *36*
12:35–37 *36*
12:38–40 *37–38*
12:38–44 *168*
12:41–44 *38*
13:1 *41*
13:1–4 *42*
13:1–37 *39*
13:2 *42*
13:5–13 *41–42*
13:7–8 *43*
13:9–13 *76*
13:10 *43*

13:14 *45*
13:14–18 *45*
13:14–23 *41, 44*
13:19–23 *45*
13:24–25 *46*
13:24–27 *41, 46*
13:28–32 *46*
13:30 *47*
13:31 *47*
13:32 *47*
13:33–37 *41, 48*
14:1 *4*
14:1–2 *3*
14:3 *3, 4*
14:3–9 *2*
14:9 *4*
14:10–11 *3, 54*
14:12–16 *60*
14:12–32 *59*
14:17 *61*
14:18–21 *63*
14:21 *65*
14:22–25 *69*
14:27–31 *72*
14:31 *101*
14:32–42 *81*
14:34 *172*
14:34–36 *82*
14:36 *83*
14:38 *85*
14:41 *85*
14:42 *85–86*
14:43 *86*
14:43–52 *85*
14:48–49 *88*
14:49 *65*
14:50 *85*
14:51–52 *89*
14:53–55 *94*
14:53–65 *97*
14:61 *106*
14:62 *98, 106*
14:66–72 *100*

14:71 *101*
15:1a *100*
15:1b–5 *110*
15:2 *111*
15:6–15 *113*
15:16–19 *120*
15:20–23 *121*
15:20–47 *119*
15:21 *121*
15:24 *124*
15:24–32 *122*
15:25 *120*
15:27 *124*
15:29–30 *130*
15:32 *131*
15:33 *120*
15:33–34 *132*
15:33–37 *132*
15:34 *90–91,
127, 133, 177*
15:38 *136, 178*
15:38–41 *135*
15:39 *136, 178*
15:40–41 *130*
15:42–45 *137*
15:46 *89*
15:46–47 *138*
16:1–8 *143, 145*
16:5 *89*
16:8 *146*
16:9–20 *148*

Luke
2:34–35 *130*
5:1–11 *152*
5:10 *152*
6:27 *88*
6:28 *129, 177*
6:29 *125*
6:35 *125*
7:36–50 *3*
8:2 *148*
10:25–37 *34*

12:15 *6*
12:50 *128*
13:1 *113*
13:6–9 *15*
13:32 *112*
19:28–24:53 *xiii*
19:28–40 *1*
19:29–35 *6*
19:36–38 *9*
19:37–44 *165*
19:39–40 *10*
19:40 *11*
19:41–44 *10*
19:42 *10*
19:45–48 *18*
20:1–19 *28*
20:1–47 *28*
20:9–19 *29*
20:20–26 *32*
20:27–40 *33*
20:41–44 *36*
20:45–47 *37*
21:1–4 *38*
21:5–7 *41–42*
21:5–36 *39*
21:8–19 *41–42*
21:20 *45, 70*
21:20–23 *45*
21:20–24 *41, 44*
21:25–28 *41, 46*
21:29–33 *46*
21:34–36 *41, 48*
22:1–6 *53*
22:3 *54*
22:3–6 *54*
22:7 *59*
22:7–13 *60*
22:8 *60*
22:14–16 *61*
22:14–20 *68*
22:17–20 *69*
22:19 *68*
22:20 *70*
22:21–23 *63*

22:24–30 *71, 171*
22:24–38 *71*
22:31 *73*
22:31–34 *101, 171*
22:38 *59*
22:40 *85*
22:40–46 *81*
22:42 *173*
22:44 *82, 172*
22:46 *85*
22:47–53 *85*
22:51 *88*
22:53 *90*
22:54 *94, 97*
22:54–62 *174*
22:55–65 *100*
22:61 *101*
22:66–71 *100*
22:67–70 *100*
23:1–5 *110*
23:2 *110*
23:3 *111*
23:4 *111*
23:6–12 *112*
23:13–25 *113*
23:26–31 *122*
23:26–33 *121*
23:26–54 *119*
23:33 *124*
23:33b–43 *122*
23:34 *124–25, 128, 139, 177*
23:36 *131*
23:39 *131*
23:39–43 *177*
23:40 *131*
23:41 *131*
23:42 *131*
23:43 *127, 131*
23:44 *132*
23:44–46 *132*
23:45 *136*
23:45–49 *135*

23:46 *128, 135*
23:47 *136*
23:48 *137*
23:49 *130*
23:50–52 *137*
23:53–56 *138*
24:1–8 *145*
24:1–53 *143*
24:12 *147*
24:13–32 *150*
24:13–49 *179*
24:19–21 *179*
24:25–27 *179*
24:31 *180*
24:33–49 *150*
24:34 *149*
24:44–48 *153*
24:50–53 *154*

John

1:29 *66*
1:36 *66*
1:39 *120*
1:40–42 *101*
2:13–22 *19*
2:19 *97*
3 *178*
4:7 *60*
4:25–26 *11*
4:34 *128, 135, 178*
4:52 *120*
6:15 *54*
7 *178*
7:5 *154*
8:44 *98*
10:8 *115*
11:53 *19*
12:1–8 *2, 164*
12:3 *4, 164*
12:4 *62*
12:4–5 *4*
12:4–6 *105*
12:4–8 *54*

12:5 *5*
12:6 *5, 62*
12:7 *5*
12:8 *6*
12:12–13 *9*
12:12–19 *1, 6*
12:12–21:25 *xiii*
12:14–15 *7*
12:16 *11*
12:19 *11*
12:20–36 *11*
13:1 *61*
13:1–15 *170*
13:1–17 *61*
13:1–20 *61*
13:1–17:26 *59*
13:2 *61*
13:6–9 *62*
13:8 *62, 170*
13:10 *170*
13:14 *62*
13:18 *64*
13:21–30 *63*
13:25–26 *64*
13:27 *5, 61, 73, 90, 105*
13:34 *59*
14 *75*
14–16 *75*
14:1–4 *75*
14:1–31 *74*
14:1–16:33 *74*
14:5–7 *75*
14:8–11 *75*
14:12–14 *75*
14:15–17 *172*
14:15–31 *75*
14:16–20 *75*
14:21 *75*
14:23 *75*
14:26–27 *75*
14:27 *172*
15:1–11 *75*
15:1–17 *75*

15:12–17 *75*
15:18–16:4 *43, 75*
15:19 *115*
15:26–27 *75–76, 172*
16:5–16 *75*
16:5–33 *76*
16:7–15 *172*
16:33 *76*
17 *76, 81*
17:1–5 *76*
17:1–26 *74, 76*
17:4 *128, 135, 178*
17:6–19 *77*
17:12 *88*
17:16 *153*
17:20–26 *77*
18:1–11 *85*
18:2 *82*
18:3 *86*
18:3–12 *174*
18:6 *87*
18:8 *87*
18:12–27 *94, 96*
18:13 *94*
18:17 *94*
18:24 *97*
18:25–27 *94, 100*
18:28–38 *110*
18:31 *110–11*
18:33–37 *111*
18:38 *111, 117*
18:39–19:16 *113*
19 *178*
19:4 *117*
19:6 *117*
19:12 *117*
19:12–16 *176*
19:14 *120*
19:15 *115, 176*
19:17 *121*
19:17–42 *119*

19:18–27 *122*
19:19–22 *129, 177*
19:20 *129*
19:23–24 *124*
19:25 *130*
19:25–27 *130*
19:26–27 *126*
19:28 *127–28, 135*
19:28–30 *132*
19:30 *128, 135, 178*
19:31–37 *137*
19:31–38 *135*
19:38–42 *178*
19:39–42 *138*
20:1 *130, 145*
20:1–21:25 *143*
20:2 *146*
20:2–8 *146*
20:2–9 *146*
20:7 *147*
20:8 *147*
20:11–18 *148*
20:12 *148*
20:19–22 *153*
20:19–23 *150*
20:24–29 *151*
20:28 *151–52*
21:1–25 *152*
21:2 *180*
21:15–19 *180*
21:15–21 *153*
21:18–19 *105*

Acts
1:3 *144*
1:9–12 *154*
1:16–19 *101, 103*
1:18 *103*
2:23–36 *xiii*
2:33–36 *36*
3:13–26 *xiii*

3:14 *139*
4:1–22 *43, 157*
4:11 *31*
7 *111*
7:54–60 *125*
7:59–60 *140*
7:60 *129*
9:4 *87*
17:30–31 *158*
22:7 *87*
23:23 *86*
24:10–27 *43*
25:1–26:32 *43*

Romans

1:4 *159*
1:5 *43*
1:8 *43*
3:25 *134*
6:4–11 *158*
8:34 *36*
10:18 *43*
13:1–7 *33*
13:8–10 *35*
15:19 *43*
15:23 *43*
16:13 *121*
16:26 *43*

1 Corinthians

2:6–8 *126*
2:8 *129*
3:16–17 *166*
5:7 *66*
8:1 *49*
11:23–26 *69*
11:26 *78*
15:1–7 *xiii*
15:5 *149*
15:6–7 *153*
15:20 *136*
15:20–58 *34*

15:25 *36*
15:35–49 *152*
15:35–58 *180*
15:54–58 *160*
15:55 *128*

2 Corinthians

3:18 *158*
5:17 *158*
5:21 *83, 91, 134*
11:24–25 *43*
12:3–4 *132*
12:4 *127*

Galatians

3:13 *83, 135*
5:14 *35*

Ephesians

4:20–24 *158*
6:2–3 *126*
6:18–20 *77*

Colossians

1:6 *43*
1:23 *43*
2:11–15 *159*
3:1 *36*

1 Thessalonians

4:17–18 *158*

2 Thessalonians

2:1–11 *45*
2:9–12 *46*

1 Timothy

6:3–5 *24*
6:9–10 *105*
6:10 *6*

Hebrews

1:3 *36*
1:13 *36*
2:14 *159*
6:19–20 *136*
7:25 *76*
9:3–14 *136*
10:19–20 *136*

James

2:8 *35*

1 Peter

1:13–16 *166*
2:4 *31*
2:6–7 *31*
2:13–17 *33*
2:21–23 *116, 140*
2:21–24 *129*
2:21–25 *174*
2:24 *83*
4:19 *128*
5:8 *159*

2 Peter

3:7 *47*
3:10 *47*
3:12 *47*

1 John

1:9 *62*

Revelation

1:17 *87*
2:7 *127, 132*
13:1–8 *45*
19:10 *87*
20:1–3 *160*
21:1–8 *158*
22:8 *87*